BREAKING DOWN

THE PROFIT BARRIERS
IN DISTRIBUTION

Dr. Albert D. Bates

D. M. KREG PUBLISHING

Breaking Down the Profit Barriers in Distribution

This publication is designed to provide accurate and authoritative information in regard to financial planning for distributors. It is sold with the understanding that the publisher is not engaged in rendering legal, accounting or other professional services.

ISBN: 978-0-9893578-1-4

Cover Design/Interior Layout: Ronda Taylor, www.taylorbydesign.com

Contents

Dedication

To the four ladies in my life. You continue to make me proud beyond my wildest dreams.

Acknowledgements

Since this book is based upon forty years of trial and error in financial planning, there is no way to acknowledge all of the folks who have provided assistance, motivation and much-needed questioning of all of my ideas and approaches to profitability. Thanks to all.

For this specific book, I am indebted to Jamie Adams for her untiring work on getting the text into readable form. She is probably the only person in the world who would bother going to the Danny & The Juniors Web site to make sure a footnote was correct.

Introduction:
You Really Should Read This

This book follows a very logical chain of thought connecting three important ideas.

- The overwhelming majority of distributors do not generate the profit that they should because...
- They do a lot of things that don't improve profit and don't do enough of the things that actually do improve profit, because...
- They always have. They follow the conventional wisdom.

This book is dedicated to destroying the conventional wisdom. In that regard it is overwhelmingly counterintuitive. At some point it will challenge your most fundamental beliefs about profitability such as:

- **Cash is King**—It's actually a pretender to the throne sucking life from the business.
- **Can't Sell Apples from an Empty Cart**—Way too many of your apples are rotten and nobody wants them.
- **Sales Solves All Problems**—Most firms grow in a way that lowers profit.

Because of the failure to increase profits doing business as usual, this book is designed to shake managers out of their complacency. It will do so in a style that is acerbic, cynical, mocking, taunting and belittling. In short, it will openly shame managers who don't take action to improve results.

As a counterbalance it will also be self-deprecating. As a consultant, I share equal blame for the lack of improvement in profitability. I have not been direct enough or aggressive enough to convince clients to drive improvements. I will shame myself as things unfold. In short, the style can be summed up with the classic phrase "No More Mr. Nice Guy."

I will make the readers of this book a deal. You improve profitability and I will shut up. Sounds like a great proposition for all involved. Until you improve, though, I will stay on your case. And mine.

1 The Long-Term Profit Trend: Not Bad, Not Good

Distribution has always been one of the most stable profitability sectors of the economy. Year in and year out, distributors produce reasonable profit levels. However, too often reasonable is a code word for inadequate. By any definition, distributors are in something of a profitability rut. Not a terrible rut, but a rut nonetheless.

The central tenant of this book is that a large number of distributors could produce dramatically higher profits if they can overcome the barriers that are keeping them mired in the profit rut. A "large number" is not limited to a small minority or even just a majority of distributors.

It means that *any* firm can reach high-profit status if it is willing to challenge the conventional wisdom that permeates distribution. The opportunity to break down profitability barriers is open to all. Sadly, only a few will take advantage of that opportunity. Most will follow the path of least resistance and will continue to do business as usual. Business as usual is the normal default option.

Readers interested in doing nothing and staying in a comfortable rut should stop reading now. Put this book on eBay® to recover your investment. Only readers willing to challenge every assumption about how profit is generated should read further.

For readers who do want to plow ahead, a quick note about structure. Every chapter is organized into the time-honored model of "tell 'em what you're gonna tell 'em, tell 'em, then tell 'em what you done told 'em." For Chapter One there are four sections where you are gonna be told:

- **The Profit Rut**—A review of what the profit rut looks like in distribution and the long-term management implications of the rut.
- **Winners and Losers**—A brief analysis of what allows some firms to escape the profit rut while others are mired in it forever.

- **The Barriers to Profitability**—A review of the key topics that will be addressed in the remainder of the book. Namely, the barriers that must be overcome by management.
- **A Sample Firm**—The book is as much about numbers as it is about text. That is proven by the fact that there are 35 exhibits. It is a mind-numbing figure. Readers may disagree with the conclusions in the text. The numbers, as trial lawyers like to say, speak for themselves. When the exhibits speak, readers should pay attention. This section provides a brief overview of the example firm that will be used in all of the exhibits.

The Profit Rut

Exhibit 1 examines the aggregate Return on Assets (ROA) performance for 40 lines of trade in distribution across the last 15 years.[1] ROA is profit after all expenses, but before income taxes, expressed as a percent of the total asset investment in the business. In distribution it is often referred to as ROTA (Return on Total Assets).

CFOs in particular should notice that pre-tax profit is not the same as EBITDA. The profit figure used here is before income taxes because different firms with different organizational structures pay very different tax rates. Taxes get in the way of meaningful comparisons.

However, profit is *after*—not before—interest, depreciation and amortization. The author attended (and according to his resume, graduated from) a land-grant college. Interest and depreciation were considered expenses in every course the author took. The faculty may have been second-rate, but the concepts were first-rate. Interest and depreciation are expenses.

For most profitability analysts, ROA is the single most important ratio for evaluating the overall financial performance of the firm. It measures the extent to which the firm truly has an economic model that justifies its continued existence. Firms with a low ROA are doomed to liquidation or acquisition. Firms with a high ROA are poised to take advantage of the liquidation or to be the acquirers.

Exhibit 1 traces ROA in distribution for a long enough period to reflect several years of steady growth, two unpleasant recessions and two periods of

---

[1] The Profit Planning Group conducts financial benchmarking surveys in more than 40 different lines of trade in distribution. All figures referred to as aggregates in this book represent the median results for these 40 lines of trade. That is, half of the firms did better than the results shown and half did worse.

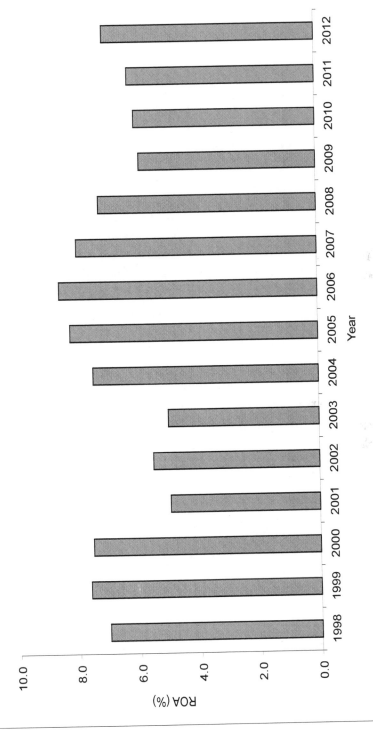

Exhibit 1
Return on Assets in Distribution by Year

recovery (one typical and one stagnant). If there is anything happening with regard to profitability, it should be discernible from such a long-term data set. It really doesn't make any difference what specific time frame is used, the same conclusion regarding the existence of a profit rut will prevail.

Unfortunately, ignoring the impact of recession and recovery, nothing happened. Well, actually, something did happen. Managers in the distribution business were 15 years older at the end of the period than at the beginning. In terms of profitability, though, firms pretty much ended up back where they started.

A 7.0% Industry

The exhibit suggests that, over time, distributor profitability is typically in the 7.0% ROA range. In good times, ROA is above that level, in bad times it is below. To use a statistical term, ROA eventually regresses back to the mean.

This steady state pattern can be viewed from two different perspectives. The "glass half full" interpretation is that distributors have delivered dependable, if unexciting, profit results consistently during the period. It is a tribute to stability.

From a financial perspective, a 7.0% ROA can be thought of as good enough. The firm generates sufficient profit to invest in new technology and expand into additional markets, albeit slowly. Firms that have celebrated their 50th anniversary in business will probably be around for the 75th.

The "glass half empty" perspective is that over the period most firms have gotten larger and much more sophisticated in nature. Apparently, the growth and sophistication have done nothing to improve profitability. Results really should have gotten better.

If a 7.0% firm could make a modest improvement and simply become, say a 10.0% firm, its financial future would become much brighter. There would be even more funds for that new technology and for more rapid expansion. If 10.0% is better than 7.0%, then 15.0% or 20.0% would be better still.

While a 7.0% ROA may be good enough to hang in, it is not what it could be with systematic effort. Much higher profit levels are attainable. Sadly, at least for the author, the glass is very much half empty.

As stated a few paragraphs before, the fundamental idea behind this book is that enhanced profitability is a realistic opportunity for any firm willing to challenge the conventional wisdom. It is time to make significant improvements in performance. Immediately would be a nice time frame.

Winners and Losers

Exhibit 1 encompasses several thousand firms from 40 different lines of trade. Within that rather large base of companies there is a lot of variation with regard to ROA. Some firms lose money; others produce an ROA in excess of 20.0%. The differences are attributable to two very different factors—structural and operational.

The concept of structural and operational differences will be discussed throughout this book. Structural factors allow the firm to "run and hide" from competition. Operational factors reflect the firm's ability to "fight for profit" after running and hiding is no longer an option.

Successful firms are good at both the structural (running and hiding) and the operational (fighting for profit) aspects of their business. Doing one well will move the firm somewhat above the fray. Both are required for real success.

This book will not be concerned with managerial excellence. The ability to manage effectively is a large topic unto itself. The entire focus is on two concepts only: (1) running and hiding and (2) fighting for profit.

- **Structural Factors**—Some lines of trade are inherently more profitable than the norm. That is, the median for the firms in these lines of trade is above the 7.0% figure for all of distribution. Alas, some lines of trade are less profitable. The median for the hard-working and intelligent folks in these industries is below 7.0%.

The differences between lines of trade are almost entirely structural in nature. Simply put, some firms are in the right place at the right time. They are in industries that allow them to run and hide almost automatically. Candidly, most firms are there by historical accident, not because of strategic brilliance on the part of management.

- **Operational Factors**—After taking advantage of every structural opportunity, firms must turn their attention to fighting for profit. Within a specific line of trade they must become the "best of breed."

It is this best of breed concept that will dominate the discussion going forward. To be best of breed requires a commitment to challenge every idea and concept about profitability that the firm currently believes in. Business as usual will not lead to higher profits in any line of trade.

Structural Factors

Operating issues involve ongoing, day-to-day activities, such as driving adequate sales and controlling pricing. Structural issues are much more episodic in character. They involve finding niches or places to hide.

Operational factors will carry the day going forward. Probably 95% of the discussion will be focused there. However, it is important to examine structural differences for a few paragraphs.[2] Doing so requires one of the many bad analogies that will torment the reader throughout the book.

Being born into the House of Windsor really helps in English society. Similarly, being in the right line of trade in distribution in North America also helps. As it turns out, the House of Windsor is a limited-entry environment for English citizens. Switching from a low-ROA line of trade to a high-ROA one is not a lot easier. Everybody is forced to play it the way it lays.

However, being in a low-profit industry does not entirely preclude the ability to run and hide. The factors that increase profits for *all* firms in those lucky lines of trade can be used on a limited basis by *individual* firms in every line of trade.

Structural differences can be summed up quickly and easily. Structural issues shield the firm from direct competition. Firms without direct competition on a day-to-day basis generate higher profits almost automatically as they have a quasi-monopoly. Even the author (probably) couldn't mess it up.

There are many structural factors that lead to higher profits in individual industries. On that long list of factors, two rise to the top. They overwhelm everything else. It should always be remembered that both of them can be applied to individual firms as well as industries.

- **Barriers to Entry**—If there are barriers of any sort associated with getting into an industry, then the firms already in that industry typically enjoy higher profits. Barriers can be legal (outright prohibition from entry all the way to stringent tests for entry), the level of technical sophistication required, the size of the capital investment necessary for entry, or any number of other factors that would cause most potential competitors to shy away. Barriers can also exist when industries are considered socially unattractive or where potential legal liabilities appear to be likely.

- **Commoditization**—Commodity-based industries always face the specter of intense price competition which severely limits profitability. Firms with unique, highly differentiated products generate higher profits, almost automatically.

---

[2] A brilliant and detailed discussion of structural factors is contained in Albert D. Bates, *Profit Myths in Wholesale Distribution*, National Association of Wholesaler-Distributors Institute for Distribution Excellence, 2008.

These run and hide factors will be sprinkled randomly through the book when their application to individual firms warrants investigation. Until then, the discussion will be focused on operational factors.

The Ongoing Challenges to Profitability: The Operational Factors

Moving from "just typical" to best of breed in a particular line of trade is a journey that every firm should want to take. The challenge in driving higher profit is that the correct path to take on that journey is far from obvious. Finding the correct path is made much more difficult by the omnipresent "conventional wisdom."

Conventional wisdom involves blindly adhering to the concepts and ideas that produced the profit rut to begin with. It is blind obedience to Einstein's famous observation about "doing the same thing over and over and expecting different results."[3] Conventional wisdom has two very ugly parents.

The first is an acceptance of ideas and concepts that are repeated over and over simply *because* they are repeated over and over. If everybody says that "Cash is King" then it must be true. Every one of the oft-repeated concepts will be challenged here.

The second ugly parent is the old war cry of "We have always done it this way." If firms have always done it this way and are in a profit rut, then maybe a new way is an approach whose time has come.

Before moving forward the author should proffer a much-needed mea culpa. The author, like every other brilliant distribution consultant, does not have to actually manage a distribution business. As Teddy Roosevelt so aptly described it in a famous speech:

> *It is not the critic who counts; not the man who points out how the strong man stumbles, or where the doer of deeds could have done them better. The credit belongs to the man who is actually in the arena...*[4]

---

[3] Like many brilliant quotes it is improperly attributed. There is no evidence that Einstein ever said it and a lot of evidence that he did not. Why let that get in the way, though? The first documented use of the phrase is in a pamphlet by Narcotics Anonymous in 1981.

[4] Theodore Roosevelt in a speech entitled *Citizenship in a Republic,* delivered in Paris on April 23, 1910. This quote should be remembered whenever it appears the author is whining. The author is really trying to help, albeit from as far away as possible. This quote also allows the author to appear to be erudite.

With the apology stated, the author—in the role of shameless critic—could not help but notice that distributors tend to make a number of key mistakes on a recurring basis. Those mistakes need to be addressed in a positive way. Not to criticize, but to suggest opportunities for improvement.

Over the course of 30 years of analyzing financial results in more than 40 lines of trade in distribution (and another 100 industries outside of distribution), the author has identified six issues that seem to get in the way of higher profitability. These issues will be the focus of the remaining chapters in this book.

- **Misunderstanding the CPVs**—A small number of performance factors, what are commonly called the Critical Profit Variables, drive profitability. When these factors can be combined properly, profit surges ahead. When they are not combined properly profit lags well behind its potential level. The most fundamental profit mistake made in distribution is not managing the CPVs in an effective manner.

- **Sales Myopia**—Sales is the lifeblood of any business. However, reliance on sales growth to solve all problems is a serious addiction. As strange as it may seem, rapid growth is not always better than slower growth. Firms need to find the Goldilocks level of growth that is just right for sustained profit improvement.

- **Gross Margin Defeatism**—Generating an adequate gross margin (also called gross profit) is essential for success. Far too many firms have taken the perspective that it's a price competitive jungle out there. As a result they have given up on improving gross margin, often without even realizing they have done so. They have, de facto, given up on producing higher profit.

- **Sales Force Abdication**—Sales management is the final frontier of profit improvement. For a multiplicity of reasons, poor performance by the sales staff is allowed in a way that would not be tolerated in any other position in the firm. It is essential to get control over the sales force without squeezing out the enthusiasm that salespeople need to perform.

- **Investment Strangulation**—Distributors are chronically short of cash. This reality leads to a wide range of short-term expedients to conserve cash. Such expedients almost always destroy profit in the long run. Distributors must find a way to have the golden egg of cash without killing the profit goose. (Stay calm; the metaphors will get even worse.)

- **Overbudgeting**—Stop the presses. A financial book attacking the budgeting process? Unbelievable, but true. Some noble efforts to increase financial sophistication have actually made the planning process overly complicated and of limited value. Time for a dose of "less is more."

If these six issues can be addressed properly, almost any distributor should be able to increase its ROA. However, there is one sad caveat. Nowhere will the term "easy" be employed. Terms like realistic, attainable, doable and achievable will be used in its stead. "Easy" will be exiled to the books on marketing via social media.

One last bit of business before getting into the details of driving higher profit. It is necessary to have a firm to play with. That firm is Mountain View Distributing.

The Sample Firm: Mountain View Distributing

Distributors range in sales size from less than a million to several billion dollars. Gross margin percentages, depending upon the industry, range from around 5.0% to over 40.0%. No one sample company can reflect all of these firms with absolute accuracy.

Luckily, firms big and small, high gross margin and low gross margin, all face the same profit barriers. A mid-range sample company can serve to demonstrate actions that every firm should think about. That sample company will be referred to here as Mountain View Distributing.[5]

The various financial and operating characteristics of the firm are shown in **Exhibit 2**. Financially astute readers should feel free to skim or even skip this section. However, references to Exhibit 2 will permeate the remainder of the book. A basic knowledge of Mountain View will prove helpful.

Income Statement

The firm generates sales revenue of $20.0 million. This is a nice round number that makes the discussion easy to follow. Mid-range firms can identify with it. Large firms can think of it as a significant branch. Small firms can view it as a long-term goal or can subtract a zero.

The firm's gross margin (or gross profit) percentage is 25.0% of revenue. That means the firm buys things for $0.75, sells them for $1.00 and keeps $0.25.

---

[5] Readers who have suffered through multiple convention presentations by the author have seen the Mountain View moniker numerous times. The name Mountain View is used because the author lives in Colorado and residents of that state think names like Mountain View are really swift. Remember that our ancestors were not smart enough to get to California.

Exhibit 2
Financial and Operating Results
Mountain View Distributing, Inc.

Income Statement	Dollars	Percent
Net Sales	$20,000,000	100.0
Cost of Goods Sold	15,000,000	75.0
Gross Margin	5,000,000	25.0
Expenses		
Payroll and Fringe Benefits	3,000,000	15.0
All Other Expenses	1,500,000	7.5
Total Expenses	4,500,000	22.5
Profit Before Taxes	500,000	2.5
Income Taxes (30.0% of PBT)	150,000	0.8
Profit After Taxes	$350,000	1.8

Supplemental Expense Analysis	Dollars	Percent
Fixed Expenses (overhead)	$3,500,000	17.5
Variable Expenses	1,000,000	5.0
Total	$4,500,000	22.5

Partial Balance Sheet	Dollars	Percent
Cash	$125,000	2.0
Accounts Receivable	2,187,500	35.0
Inventory	2,500,000	40.0
Other Current Assets	62,500	1.0
Total Current Assets	4,875,000	78.0
Fixed Assets	1,375,000	22.0
Total Assets	$6,250,000	100.0
Accounts Payable	$1,000,000	

Operating Metrics

Number of Employees	50
Sales per Employee	$400,000
Average Transaction	$500
GMROI*	200.0%
Return on Assets	8.0%

* Gross Margin Return on Inventory. A detailed explanation of the term is in Chapter Two.

The firm's pre-tax bottom line is 2.5% of revenue. The numbers that were so large at the top of the income statement are so small by the time you get to the bottom. The $20.0 million in revenue only results in $500,000 of pre-tax profit.

On the income statement there is one other critical point. It involves the expense structure. The overwhelming majority of expenses are payroll and associated fringe benefits (FICA, Medicare, workers' compensation, health insurance and 401(k) contributions). Distribution is a service business. Service businesses require people to provide the service. Those people have to get paid.

For Mountain View exactly two-thirds of all expenses are payroll related. The other one-third is, by definition, everything else. This includes rent, utilities, interest, gas and oil, bad debts, depreciation and anything else one can think of.

This 67% payroll/33% everything else ratio holds throughout distribution. It may go to 60/40 or 70/30 in some industries, but not much beyond. Payroll is the name of the game.

This leads to one important point. Any and every discussion of expenses will have to zero in on payroll. At no time will the author suggest a slash and burn approach to payroll. The idea of better payroll control will be mentioned early and often, though.

Supplemental Expense Analysis

At various points it will be necessary to utilize a different view of expenses than payroll versus everything else. Those points will be when the firm increases or decreases its sales volume during the course of a *single year*. This supplemental approach to expenses involves re-categorizing them into fixed expenses and variable expenses.

This second expense concept has the potential to bog down a discussion that is already moving at a glacial pace. With any luck, the fixed and variable concepts can be disposed of in short order with two of the author's world-famous bullet points and a few supporting paragraphs.

- **Fixed Expenses**—These are overhead expenses or the costs associated with getting ready to sell something. The real key is that they only change when management takes an action. If the CFO is given a (richly deserved) raise, then the fixed expenses have increased by the size of the pay raise. During the unpleasant shrinking of many distributors during the Great Recession, every dollar of payroll reduction was a dollar of fixed expense reduction.

- **Variable Expenses**—These are items which increase or decrease at the same rate that sales volume increases or decreases. They tend to do so almost automatically. The most obvious example is sales commissions. As the sales force generates more sales, they receive more in compensation.

Clearly, this is a simplification. Some variable expenses may be associated with the amount of gross margin; say paying commissions based on gross margin rather than sales. Some variable expenses may be related to physical activity rather than sales dollars. For example, if the firm had to process a lot of returned merchandise, warehouse costs would rise even though sales did not. The simplification is not going to distort anything, so please live with it.

For Mountain View it is assumed that fixed expenses are $3,500,000. That is, the firm starts the year knowing it will have to incur that amount in expenses unless it takes some actions to drive the number up or down. When next year starts the fixed expenses for the year will almost certainly increase due to pay raises and the like. For this year, the baseline figure is $3,500,000.

Variable expenses are assumed to be 5.0% of revenue. Every time revenue goes up or down, variable expenses go up or down just as fast and remain exactly 5.0% of sales.

Please notice the term *assumed* relating to both fixed and variable expenses in the two previous paragraphs. The breakout of expenses into the fixed and variable categories is always an estimation process. Luckily a reasonable estimate is all that is required. None of the conclusions about profitability will change if the estimates are off a little (or even off a lot for that matter) in the designation of fixed versus variable.

Partial Balance Sheet

The investment portion of the exhibit looks primarily at the asset side of the balance sheet. That side is enough to provide some important observations. First, the firm does not have a lot of cash. Firms with lots of cash are called banks.

Second, accounts receivable and inventory are the big enchiladas when it comes to asset investment. Whether they are too big will be discussed further down the road. For now, just note that 75.0% of total assets are tied up in these two items.

The liabilities side of the balance sheet will be blissfully ignored here. It is really not that big of an omission even though it may seem like it at first glance. There are no CPVs hiding in the liability bushes, so why waste time there?

Actually, there is a memo line for Accounts Payable. At present Mountain View owes its suppliers $1.0 million. This item, combined with the fact that the firm has only $125,000 in cash does cause shortness of breath in some managers. It shouldn't. The situation is very manageable, as will be discussed in Chapter Six.

No other liabilities deserve attention. For the few readers (mostly accountants) who are infuriated by the lack of a complete statement of liabilities, a word of advice: Write your own book. The rest of us, like the country song says, gotta travel on.

Operating Metrics

The very bottom part of the exhibit provides a few details regarding some key operating metrics for the company, including sales per employee, average transaction size and GMROI (whatever that is). Such ratios are common coin for management of most distribution entities. Again, they will be examined in more detail as the book picks up speed, assuming it ever does.

Finally, for computational ease, Mountain View has been made slightly more profitable than the 7.0% ROA level that was presented in the rant that started the chapter. Mountain View has an 8.0% ROA which is only a smidgen above the typical result for distributors as a whole. Using 7.0% for an ROA creates an arithmetic nightmare which will cause some very non-round numbers to get in the way of the discussion.

Moving Forward to Chapter Two

Mountain View can be described, in highly technical parlance, as doing okay. In that regard, the firm is a lot like most distributors. There is no threat to survival, but the results don't generate the funds necessary to move ahead of the competition. It is good enough to stay in a nice, comfortable rut.

For firms that want to escape the rut and become best of breed there is a need to try something different. That something different will require challenging the conventional wisdom. It will necessitate some important changes in performance. The next chapter will focus on where those changes should be made. The remaining chapters will then outline how they can be implemented.

Takeaways from Chapter One

- The typical distributor produces a profit level that will allow it to stay in business until the end of civilization. The firms on the lower rung of profitability are at risk, but the typical firm is not.

- The typical firm is also in a profit rut. Staying in business is a great goal, but not good enough. The rut is created by continuing to do business as usual.
- Continuing to do business as usual in the future may cause more firms to drop down to the lower rung. To mix metaphors in mid-discussion, they may "go gentle into that good night."
- The managers of distribution firms are *not* ignorant oafs. They are running complicated businesses with a rising level of sophistication. The overwhelming percentage of managers that the author has met are incredibly smart dudes and dudettes.
- Managers are being told a lot of things about how to run those businesses by consultants, bankers, business acquaintances, suppliers and the authors of books on distributor economics. A lot of what they are being told is contradictory. Even worse, a lot of what they are being told is flat out wrong. There is a large pile of misinformation and bad advice available to distributors.

Much of what follows is counterintuitive. Please read it with an open mind. Don't accept conventional wisdom just because it is often repeated.

Time to drive higher profits. Head to the next page.

2 Misunderstanding the CPVs

Every management decision and every employee action in distribution impacts profit through what are commonly called the CPVs—the Critical Profit Variables.[6] That is, decisions and actions cause sales to go up or down or expenses to rise or fall, or other of the CPVs to change. As a final result, profit changes.

Despite the complexity of operating a distribution business, there are only five really important CPVs:

- **Sales Volume**—The revenue generated by the firm.
- **Gross Margin**—The bag of dollars left over from sales after paying for the merchandise (and possibly services) sold by the firm. In some firms this is referred to as Gross Profit.
- **Expenses**—The costs of operating the business. As stated before, payroll (fully loaded) is the major expense category. Anything else associated with running the business also is included here—rent, utilities, interest, the cost of the insightful decision to purchase this book. Anything and everything else.
- **Accounts Receivable**—The investment associated with selling merchandise to customers on terms and then waiting for them to take their own sweet time to pay.
- **Inventory**—The value of the merchandise carried to support sales.

There are some other factors that are impacted by managerial decisions and actions, such as the investment in equipment and machinery. For manufacturers such an investment would be an additional CPV. For distributors it is

---

[6] The Critical Profit Variables (CPVs) are sometimes referred to as Key Profit Drivers (KPDs) or Key Profit Indicators (KPIs). The terms are interchangeable. Using different terms allows consultants to present very old wine in what appears to be a brand new bottle.

one of the PPVs (Puny Profit Variables). Distributors must focus on the big five. Notice the term *must*.

This chapter is organized into three sections:

- **The Hierarchy of the CPVs**—Some of the CPVs are more important than others. This section will attempt to set priorities based upon profit analysis rather than conjecture or whim.

- **CPV Trade-offs**—Every one of the CPVs cannot be maximized at the same time. In almost every decision, one of the CPVs must be sacrificed for the greater good. This section will introduce the trade-off process.

- **A Brief Sojourn into the World of GMROI**—An example of how the failure to evaluate trade-offs properly causes things to go awry despite the best intentions of all involved.

The Hierarchy of the CPVs

Everybody agrees that the CPVs are, well...the critical profit variables. Where disagreement—and the occasional fist fight—emerges is in determining which of the CPVs is most important. Even within the big five, every factor can't be equal.

Setting a hierarchy is critical. If companies don't put their effort where the payoff is greatest, then profit will not improve. Luckily a brief review of the stockpile of business maxims helps develop the hierarchy:

- Nothing happens until somebody sells something.

- Every dollar of revenue in your business is the result of a pricing decision.

- Inventory is the largest investment in most businesses. Controlling inventory is the key to success.

- Expense control is actually much more powerful than sales in driving higher profits.

- The purchasing department is the one key area of your business where dramatic profit improvements can be made.

In short, *everything* is most important. Or at least everything is most important to somebody.

This was referred to in the previous chapter as a large pile of bad information. This does not mean the authors of the tomes quoted anonymously above are not incredibly smart folks with a sincere desire to help firms be more successful. What is does mean is that everybody filters information through their own kidneys.

If you are a sales consultant, sales are your life. You know for an unassailable fact that sales volume is the most important factor in the business. For inventory consultants, inventory is the most important factor. Candidly, though, if you are an inventory consultant your life is probably pretty dull.

The reality is that everything can't be most important or even above average in importance.[7] There must be some hierarchy involved. That hierarchy must be specific to distribution, not to banks or pizza parlors.

Luckily, good old Mountain View Distributing can be utilized to develop that hierarchy. It is absolutely essential to note that what is good for Mountain View is good for every other distributor, including your firm. The exact numbers will be different, but the hierarchy will not.

The CPVs can be ranked for Mountain View with regard to their impact on Return on Assets (ROA). As a quick reminder, ROA is pre-tax profit expressed as a percent of total assets. It is the single most important measure of profitability ever developed.

The ROA analysis will be conducted in four exhibits, creatively labeled Exhibit 3 through Exhibit 6. For readers with inquiring minds that want to know, a detailed proof of the exhibits is provided in Appendix A. For the moment assume that the author actually knows something and consider only the four exhibits and the text that supports them. Feel free to go forward to Appendix A when done.

All of the exhibits are identical in structure. Once the concept behind one exhibit is understood, the rest are automatically in the bag. To make sure there is complete understanding of the structure, prepare to spend some quality time with **Exhibit 3**.

Gross Margin

The exhibit (like all of the others) measures ROA on the vertical axis. The intersection point on that graph is 8.0%, which is where Mountain View is as of this moment. Mountain View is slightly above the long-term ROA level of 7.0% for all of distribution. That is still not knocking 'em dead.

On the horizontal axis in every exhibit, Mountain View will be making a series of percentage improvements in one of the CPVs. In Exhibit 3 that improvement is in the gross margin dollars that the firm is generating. The improvements range from 0.0% (for the slothful) to 25.0%. A 25.0% improvement in anything, including gross margin, is a whopping big change.

---

[7] Devotees of Garrison Keillor will remember that in Lake Wobegon every child is above average in intelligence. Keep G.K. in mind when reading business books.

Even Tom Peters would blush.[8]

The resulting graph demonstrates what happens to ROA as the improvements are made. For gross margin the line slopes upward to the right at a fairly rapid rate. Improvements in gross margin cause ROA to increase quickly.

Exhibit 3 notes on the horizontal axis that the percentage increases in gross margin are generated without increasing sales. That means the firm is producing a 5.0% increase in gross margin dollars on the existing $20.0 million of sales volume.

The easiest way to conceive of this is that the firm is selling the same quantity of merchandise at the same prices as before. Sales volume remains $20.0 million. However, the firm is now buying merchandise cheaper. Therefore, on the same sales volume the firm is generating 5.0% to 25.0% more gross margin dollars.

Two caveats are important in all of the graphs. They involve the time frame being analyzed and the impact of the action on the other CPVs.

Time Frame—All of the graphs are for the current year only. For example, Exhibit 3 describes what *would have happened* to ROA if the firm had generated anywhere from 0.0% to 25.0% more gross margin dollars than it actually did this year. Next year things will change, so a new graph will be needed. It is an extremely useful graph, but it must be limited to this year.

Impact on the Other CPVs—Changing one of the CPVs (like gross margin) might cause one of the other CPVs to change also. To be considered in the analysis, that additional change must be one that happens automatically. It can't be an arbitrary change even if that arbitrary change seems logical.

For example as gross margin dollars are increased on existing sales (Exhibit 3) it might be logical to assume that expenses would increase. The buying staff might have to be increased to find those opportunistic purchasing situations that are driving gross margin up.

This is a logical assumption, but is also blatantly arbitrary. The graphs are driven by the CPVs themselves and nothing else, unless that something else happens automatically.

These two assumptions are only minor limitations (or possibly irritations). The graph in Exhibit 3 clearly reflects the impact that increasing gross margin dollars has on the ROA the firm produces. It is a steep line. In point of fact, it is the mother of all lines. No other CPV drives ROA up as fast as increasing the

---

[8] Tom Peters was the leading proponent of making gigantic changes quickly in business. See Tom Peters and Robert H. Waterman, Jr., *In Search of Excellence*, 1982. Despite its breathless tone, the book should be on every manager's bookshelf.

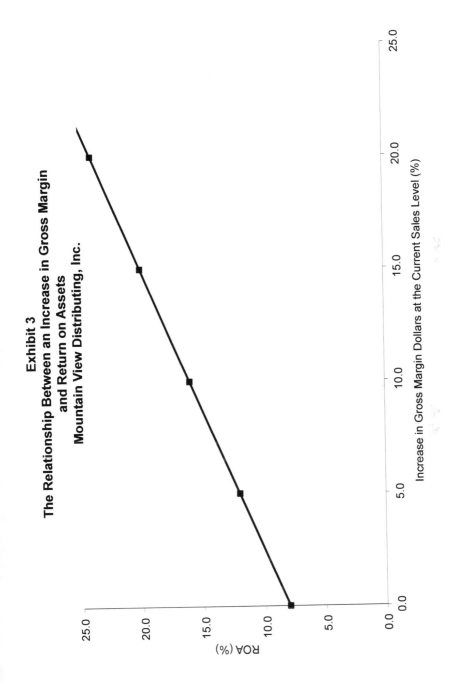

Exhibit 3
The Relationship Between an Increase in Gross Margin and Return on Assets
Mountain View Distributing, Inc.

gross margin dollars. Gross margin should be priority number one for every distributor. Wow, a conclusion about the CPVs already.

Sales Volume

Exhibit 4 applies the same analytical process to sales volume. It is still the current year and the percentage increases in sales displayed (up to 25.0%) are over and above what the firm *actually* did. It is a classic series of "what ifs," just like Exhibit 3.

The increase in sales is made while holding the gross margin at 25.0% of revenue. This means that when sales increase by 5.0%, the total dollars of gross margin generated also increase by 5.0%.

In addition, the expense structure of fixed and variable remains in place. Variable expenses are 5.0% of the increased sales, and fixed expenses remain constant—it is still this year. At the 25.0% sales increase level the employees may be begging for additional personnel to help do all of the extra work. Logical—but arbitrary—so it doesn't happen.

Don't get too upset; the "no change in the other CPVs unless it is automatic" rule gets stretched a little here. The stretching is on the investment side. As sales rise, two investment factors also rise—accounts receivable and inventory.

The increase in accounts receivable is certain to happen. As the firm sells more, it is automatically owed more by its customers. With 5.0% more sales there is a 5.0% increase in accounts receivable. There is no assumption stretching yet.

Inventory is something of a different matter. Ultimately, an increase in sales will require more inventory. At the left side of the graph, though, it might be possible to do just a little more sales with the same amount of inventory. Towards the right side more inventory is definitely needed, but how much more is an open issue.

In the long run, inventory will ultimately increase proportionately to sales, unless the firm installs a better inventory control system (arbitrary assumption). In the short run inventory will *probably* increase proportionately to sales. The result is an imperfect assumption, but good enough to see the concept.

The net result is a line that is steep, but one that pales in comparison to the growth in ROA due to gross margin seen in Exhibit 3. In short, from a "bang-for-the-buck" perspective, more margin on the same sales is much more powerful than increasing sales. This says nothing yet about whether or not any of

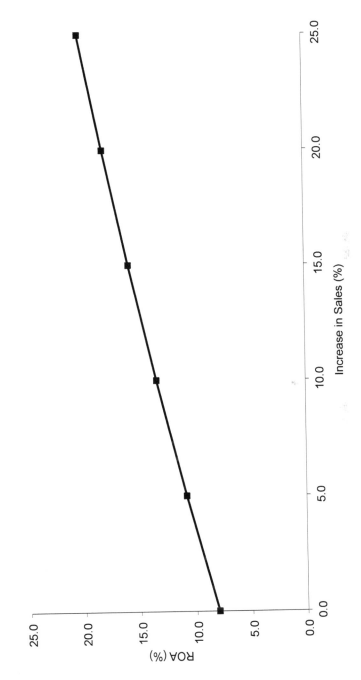

Exhibit 4
The Relationship Between a Sales Volume Increase and Return on Assets Mountain View Distributing, Inc.

this can be done. It may be impossible to increase either gross margin or sales. That conundrum will be addressed shortly.

Expenses

Exhibit 5 drops the proverbial other shoe. For most readers it will be a size 16DDD brogan. The line reflecting the ROA improvement from decreasing expenses is a lot *steeper* than the ROA line for increasing sales. That means that a 5.0% decrease in expenses does a lot more to improve ROA than a 5.0% increase in sales.

Once again there is the "no impact on the other CPVs" assumption. In this case, when expenses are reduced there is no parallel decline in sales volume. As always, a pretty good assumption for small reductions in expenses and a pretty bad assumption for large reductions.

The fact that reducing expenses has a more dramatic impact on ROA than increasing sales does not sit well with very many managers. It is just too unpleasant a thought for comfort. Most managers will simply ignore this bothersome fact and assume that it will go away. There is a phrase for this: continuing to believe the conventional wisdom.

Even managers who accept the conclusion (since it is presented so brilliantly) dislike the comparison between Exhibits 4 and 5. In the case of Sales Managers, dislike morphs into outright hatred.

The problem is that while expense control is great at increasing ROA, it has lousy public relations. From a PR perspective, expense control is viewed as better than the Ebola virus, but not as good as the United States Postal Service. To change metaphors in mid-paragraph yet again, expense reductions are always viewed as a retreat while sales increases are always viewed as a charge up San Juan Hill.

There is absolutely nothing in the exhibit that says such views can't be kept. Managers must believe in what they do. However, it must be remembered that while expense reductions are absolutely distasteful, they are very profitable.

So far the priorities are gross margin, then expenses, and finally, sales. Since some readers only get to this point while kicking and screaming, they will be forgiven if they take a quick peek at the first three sections of Appendix A and make sure the author is not lying through his teeth. The kicking and screaming is about to get worse.

Exhibit 5
The Relationship Between an Expense Reduction
and Return on Assets
Mountain View Distributing, Inc.

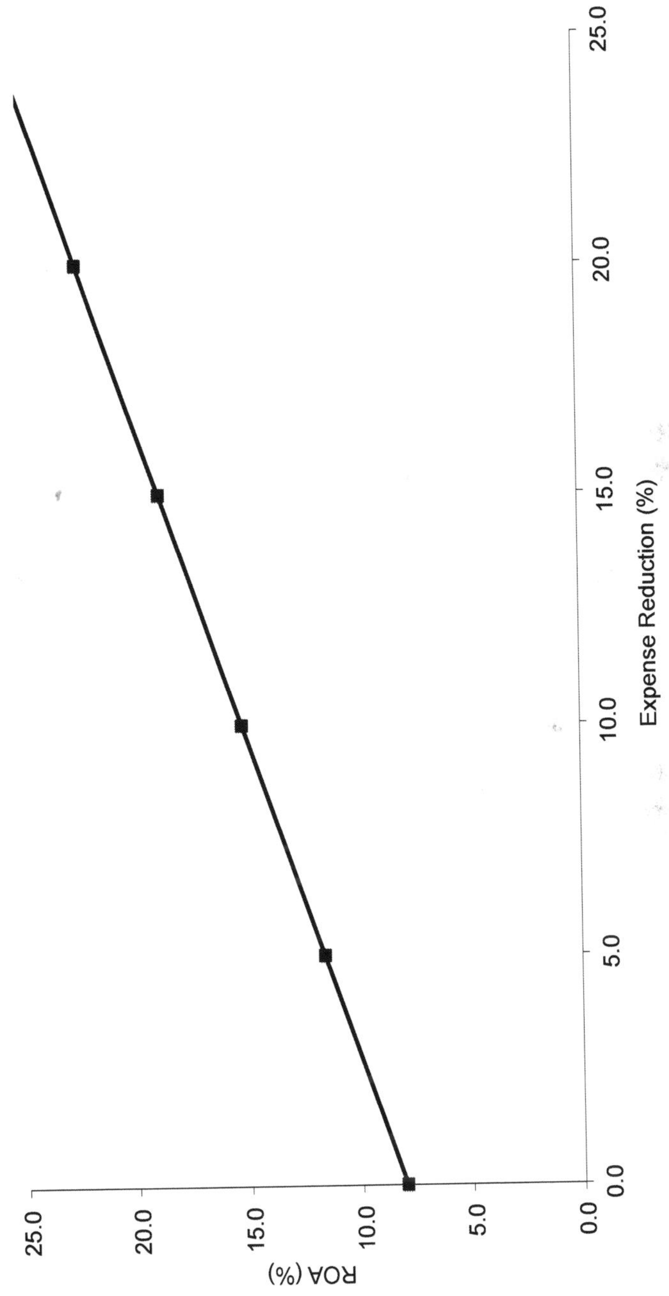

Key Investment Factors

It is now time to switch to a topic that is chock full of controversy. At its core, it is a topic that suggests much of what distributors have been doing over the course of the last five years has been wasted effort.

It is also a topic that will require a rather lengthy discussion. Namely, **Exhibit 6** indicates that reducing inventory and accounts receivable has only a miniscule impact on ROA. The graph is flatter than the beer at closing time.

Feel free to shout "That can't be right." It has been shouted before. You're not breaking new ground. Do not go so far as to close the book in disgust. The fact that the graph is flat is a point that must be understood if distributors are going to reach their full profit potential.

From a common sense perspective, lowering either inventory or accounts receivable *absolutely must* have a huge impact on ROA. This is because such a change will improve both the numerator and denominator in the ROA calculation.

Profit will rise with less investment, so the ROA numerator goes up. The asset base will decline so the denominator will go down. With two factors working at the same time, the slope of the line really should be steep. Sorry, but it isn't.

Many readers will want to go to Appendix A right now. Resist that urge. **Exhibit 7** is lifted whole cloth from Appendix A. That exhibit and the accompanying discussion will cover what is happening as succinctly as possible by focusing on inventory.

An analysis of the impact of changes in accounts receivable follows the same logic as that for inventory. It is not covered here as it would simply duplicate the inventory discussion. After reading the text supporting Exhibit 7, feel free to kick the tires of Appendix A to ensure that Graphs 3–6 are correct.

ROA Denominator—The calculation of the denominator is a lot simpler than for the numerator, so allow the author to get it out of the way first. When either inventory or accounts receivable is reduced, the firm's investment level—total assets—does, indeed, decrease. In the case of Mountain View, which has $2,500,000 in inventory (Line 7), a 10.0% reduction would reduce inventory by $250,000 (Line 9). The total assets base would decrease by the same amount, from $6,250,000 to $6,000,000 (Line 10).

So far it appears that ROA really should explode. The denominator has fallen. When the numerator rises at the same time, things will really take off.

Exhibit 6
The Relationship Between an Investment Reduction and Return on Assets
Mountain View Distributing, Inc.

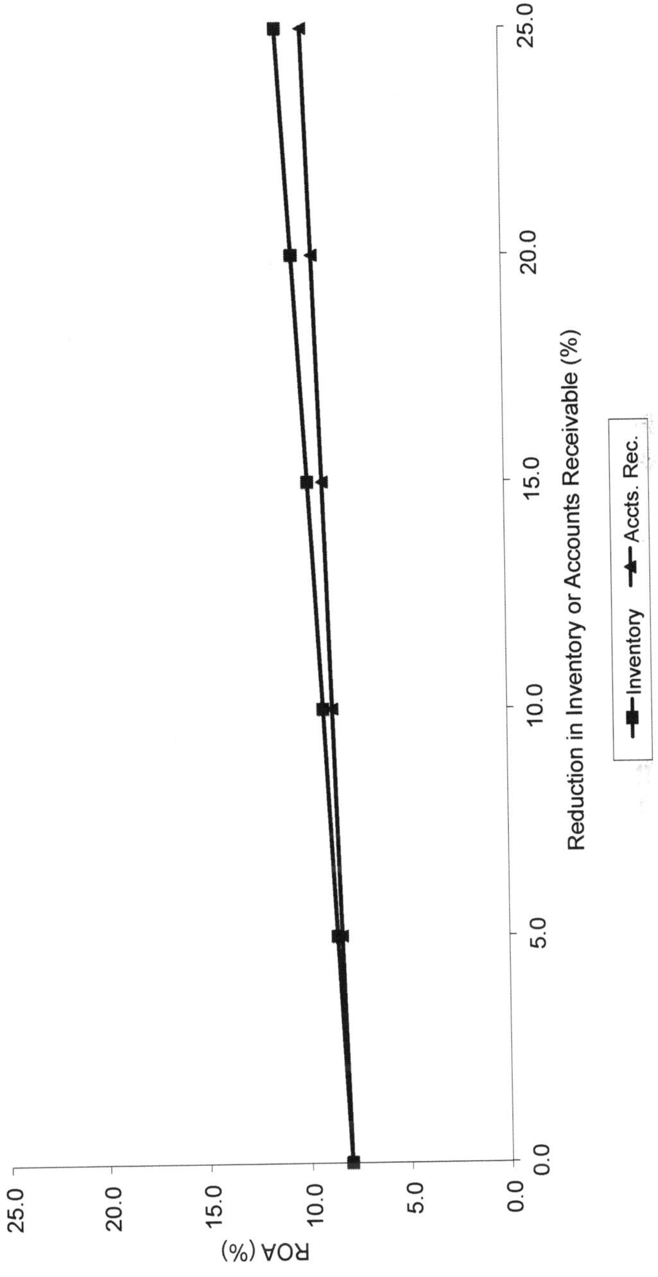

ROA Numerator—On the profit side, the reduction in investment ($250,000 less inventory) will cause expenses to go down. The magnitude of the expense reduction is based on what is called the Inventory Carrying Cost (ICC). In simplest terms, these are the expenses that arise because the firm has inventory. More importantly, they are the expenses that will go away as inventory is reduced.

The problem is that the ICC is not a single line item, but is hidden within a lot of individual line items on the income statement. Specifically it is in factors such as interest, obsolescence and a few other miscellaneous things. In short, the ICC is a legitimate metric, but has to be estimated from a lot of individual items.

The ICC is expressed as a percentage of the inventory value. In Exhibit 7, an ICC of 20.0% is assumed (Line 4). This means that every time inventory is reduced by $1.00, that reduction causes total expenses in the firm to be reduced by $0.20. This is an outrageously high ICC factor.[9] A high ICC is used to give inventory reductions every possible advantage they can have. This means that the ROA line for inventory is as steep as it could possibly be.

With the 10.0% reduction, inventory fell by the $250,000 as noted above (Line 3). A 20.0% ICC means that expenses are reduced and profit is increased by $50,000 ($250,000 times 20.0%, shown in Line 5). The new profit is equal to the old profit of $500,000 plus the cost savings from reducing inventory of $50,000, resulting in a new profit of $550,000 (Line 6).

ROA Calculation—Finally! The numerator is up and the denominator is down. *I am inventory, hear me roar in ROA numbers too big to ignore.* The new ROA of 9.2% is equal to $550,000 (new profit) divided by $6,000,000 (new total assets) (or 9.166666% for purists). That is exactly what good old Exhibit 6 indicates at the 10.0% inventory reduction point. It is an improvement, but it sure isn't much of one.

To be redundant (the author's specialty), Exhibits 6 and 7 assume that reductions in inventory do not cause other factors to change unless those changes are automatic. In point of fact, reducing either one of these could cause a significant reduction in sales. That assumption is very realistic, but still arbitrary.

---

[9] The ICC calculation and the fact that it is almost always overstated are discussed in Appendix B. It detracts from the narrative to cover it here. The Accounts Receivable Carrying Cost (ARCC not covered in the discussion above) is thrown in for good measure in Appendix B.

Exhibit 7
The Impact on ROA of a
10% Reduction in Inventory
Mountain View Distributing, Inc.

Numerator of the ROA Calculation

1	Profit Before Taxes		$500,000
2	Inventory		$2,500,000
3	10% Decrease in Inventory	[2 x 10%]	$250,000
4	Inventory Carrying Cost		20.0%
5	Increase in Profit	[3 x 4]	$50,000
6	New Profit	[1 + 5]	$550,000

Denominator of the ROA Calculation

7	Inventory	[2]	$2,500,000
8	Total Assets		$6,250,000
9	Decrease in Inventory	[3]	$250,000
10	New Total Assets	[8 - 9]	$6,000,000

ROA Calculation

11	New Profit	[6]	$550,000
12	New Total Assets	[10]	$6,000,000
13	New ROA	[11 ÷ 12]	9.2%

As every Sales Manager has opined (or whined) to every CFO, "You can't sell apples from an empty cart." Reducing inventory by simply slashing the investment for every SKU provides an unprecedented opportunity to reduce sales volume. Since the slope of Exhibit 4 (sales) is a lot steeper than the slope of Exhibit 6 (inventory), *any* reduction in inventory that causes sales to decline even slightly sends the firm on a trip to an unpleasantly warm place in a small, but well-appointed, hand-basket.

It is worth noting from a historical perspective that over the course of the last decade, many firms have made reducing their investment in inventory and accounts receivable a top priority. This has been a major contributor to the ROA rut. Sisyphus would have been proud.

Finalizing Profit Priorities

Based upon their impact on profitability, the CPV priorities for distributors should be nothing other than:

1. Gross Margin
2. Expenses
3. Sales Volume
4. Investment Levels (Inventory and Accounts Receivable)

Sometimes simply looking at the impact on profitability does not tell the whole story (the author had to bite his tongue while writing that sentence). It is entirely possible that factors that have a very large impact on profitability, such as gross margin, may be extremely difficult to improve.

It is also possible that there may be absolutely no enthusiasm within the organization for making some of the potential improvements. To experience this firsthand, run expense reductions up the old flagpole at the next manager's meeting and watch grown men and women cry.

Any profit improvement plan must consider both the highly analytical (bang for the buck) and the subjective (degree of difficulty). What no distributor should do, though, is allow the degree of difficulty to serve as a roadblock for taking action. Firms that don't at least try to improve gross margin or expenses are passing on an incredibly large profit opportunity.

CPV Trade-offs

So far the analysis has been limited to one CPV at a time. Raise sales, for example, and see what happens to ROA. Exhibits 3–7 were all handicapped by the one-at-a-time limitation.

The fun (or what financial analysts call fun) starts when the trade-offs between the different CPVs are examined. Life, as every economist will boringly tell you, is about trade-offs. Should you buy the Lamborghini or the Maserati? Wait, that decision only comes after you utilize what is in this book.

Back to the matter at hand. All of the CPVs can be evaluated in relationship to each other. This will be the sum and substance of much of the remainder of this book. To start, it is useful to understand how these trade-offs will be approached.

A great example is provided by examining the relationship between sales and inventory that was introduced earlier in this chapter. Since it was stated that sales had a large impact on profits while inventory had a small one, it would be nice to find out if that is really true when one is played against the other.

Exhibit 8
The Break-Even Point:
The Sales Decline That Will Exactly Offset
a Reduction in Expenses
Mountain View Distributing, Inc.

$$\frac{\text{Current Profit} + \text{Fixed Expenses} - \text{Expense Reduction}}{\text{Gross Margin \%} - \text{Variable Expense \%}}$$

=

$$\frac{\$500,000 + \$3,500,000 - \$50,000}{25.0\% - 5.0\%}$$

=

$$\frac{\$3,950,000}{20.0\%}$$

=

$$\$19,750,000$$

Exhibit 8 takes the information for inventory and places it in the context of a sales change. The exhibit utilizes the classic break-even formula, a tool that will prove handy in later chapters.

For readers not conversant with the break-even formula, Exhibit 8 looks like a mess of random numbers. For now, just assume the analysis is correct and follow it through to the conclusion. At some point the break-even-challenged reader should peruse Appendix C which walks through the basic process and its wide range of applications.

In Exhibit 7 a 10.0% reduction in inventory caused profit to increase by $50,000. It was suggested that possibly the inventory reduction would come at the expense of sales as the firm might be out of stock more often. The break-even formula in Exhibit 8 provides a precise look at how much sales would have to fall to destroy everything that was gained by reducing inventory.

The numerator in Exhibit 8 adds the current profit and the fixed expenses together for Mountain View. It then subtracts the expense reduction that was generated by lowering the investment in inventory. That expense reduction (profit increase) is actually subtracted because the goal is to see how far sales will have to fall to wipe out the expense improvement.

Again, if this doesn't make any sense, just keep following the discussion to its conclusion. After that, plan to curl up with Appendix C and a glass of tawny port to read about the structure of the break-even formula and how it works.

The denominator indicates that each dollar generated is not actually worth a dollar. For every $1.00 generated, $0.75 immediately goes to the suppliers of the merchandise that was sold (the gross margin is 25.0%). In addition, to paraphrase the nursery rhyme, everywhere that sales went, variable expenses were sure to follow. They continue to be 5.0% of sales. This leaves 20.0% to cover the fixed expenses and generate a profit.

In the exhibit, the firm has to cover $3,950,000 in expenses and profit with dollars that are only worth $0.20. With this set of numbers the formula demonstrates how far sales can fall before the profit improvement from lower inventory is wiped out. The answer is $19,750,000. Converting to a percentage decline, it only takes a 1.25% decline in sales to offset the profit generated by a 10.0% reduction in inventory.

The trade-off analysis is like almost every other precise financial tool. It doesn't say jack about what to do. All it can do is provide the trade-off relationship which management can then interpret as it sees fit.

That said, a 1.25% decline in sales is pretty small. The smart money leans towards the fact that inventory reductions might not be all they are cracked up to be if they are associated with *any* decline in sales.

The remaining chapters of this book deal with similar examples of trade-offs. Is it good to cut price and drive more sales volume? Should the firm provide cash discounts to customers to encourage prompt payment? Many thrilling examples will unfold in the remaining chapters. Try not to hyperventilate in anticipation.

A Brief Sojourn into the World of GMROI: A Case Study in Bad Metrics

Gross Margin Return on Inventory (GMROI) is by far the most widely used metric for evaluating inventory profitability in distribution. It is also the dumbest.

Sometimes the author is not entirely clear, so let's try again. GMROI is utterly without redeeming social value. It is the kudzu of financial metrics and needs to be eradicated. It is also the most widely-used inventory *profitability* metric in distribution. Houston, we have a problem.

GMROI is a very complicated subject. The details can't be discussed here without destroying what little flow this chapter still has. Consequently, the current discussion will follow the time-honored consultant's tradition of viewing the topic from 30,000 feet. The discussion will center on two ways in which GMROI brilliantly helps firms lower profits rather than raise them. [10]

Before jumping in, it should be noted that many readers of this book probably have never heard of GMROI (for example, branch managers and salespeople). For readers in that camp, review this section as a warning note regarding other, equally-poor metrics that you may employ. Other readers (such as buyers, department managers and merchandisers) use GMROI every day in their decision making. For you nice folks: take copious notes.

GMROI (including its evil twin, the Turn and Earn Ratio) is being discussed here as a case study because it illustrates two serious deficiencies in the way traditional analysis approaches profitability:

- **Limited Scope**—GMROI, like many other financial metrics, examines only part of an issue (for GMROI, the issue is inventory profitability) when the ability to examine the entire issue is at hand.

- **Improper Trade-offs**—GMROI makes the classic mistake of equating, and making a trade-off between, two variables that are not close to equal.

These two subjects may be a little opaque at present. That problem should be eliminated shortly.

It is worth mentioning from the start that GMROI was not designed by some financial malcontent dedicated to inflicting pain on distributors. It is a well-intentioned concept that simply does not work. It is absolute proof once again that the road to Hades really is paved with good intentions.

GMROI was designed to provide a return on investment perspective in managing inventory. That is, if ROA is really important at the total firm level, then something akin to ROA would be great for looking at individual items or suppliers. Conceptually, a great idea. The problem is that conceptual brilliance doesn't necessarily translate into functional brilliance.

The total-firm results for Mountain View can be used to illustrate the GMROI calculation. At that point it can be dissected to discern the problems. As a reminder, the firm generated (according to Exhibit 2) $5,000,000

---

[10] Folks who want to know all of the sordid details can download the white paper, *Saying Goodbye to GMROI*. It is more than a little technical. It is also as long as most chapters of this book. Be prepared for some really fun reading. It is available at profitplanninggroup.com. Go to the Seminar Materials tab and use the pull-down screen to find the white paper.

in gross margin with an inventory investment of $2,500,000. This means it had a GMROI of 200.0%. It was able to produce $2.00 of gross margin for each $1.00 invested in inventory. It is kind of like ROA in that higher is better than lower.

The Limited-Scope Problem—The limited-scope issue is that GMROI, like a lot of other metrics, only looks at a couple of aspects of a specific financial issue. Using only those aspects leads to a conclusion and a series of management actions. The use of additional information might have lead to an entirely different conclusion and different management actions.

To demonstrate this, let's consider (at the total firm level) a wonderful new opportunity the firm faces. A key supplier has agreed to carry inventory for the distributor and provide it on a just-in-time basis. This will lower the distributor's total inventory investment by 10.0%. However, the supplier will charge a (fair and reasonable) fee for this service so the firm's gross margin dollars will fall by 2.0%. Rather than looking at one supplier, let's consider the entire firm.

Doing the GMROI calculation involves two factors. The firm's gross margin falls to $4.9 million ($5.0 million times 98.0%). At the same time, inventory falls to $2.25 million ($2.5 million times 90.0%). Bingo Bob! GMROI soars from 200.0% to 217.7% ($4.9 million divided by $2.25 million). The classic GMROI approach would strongly favor this idea.

However, at the total company level there is a lot more going on than just the changes in gross margin and inventory. As only one example, there is the issue of the cost of carrying the inventory. The gross margin decline of $100,000 is a clear loss. Using an ICC of 20.0% introduced in all its splendor and glory previously means that expenses would fall by $50,000. That is the inventory reduction of $250,000 times the 20.0% ICC.

Overall, profit has actually declined by $50,000. However, the GMROI increased, implying it was a good deal. This is not a random example. In point of fact, suppliers and distributors have developed such inventory-shifting programs thousands of times over the last decade. They have almost never proved profitable, but they have increased the old GMROI.

Improper Trade-offs—The GMROI concept suggests that the firm has two *equally-good* options to drive profitability: (1) generate more gross margin dollars or, (2) lower the investment in inventory. This is so incredibly important it must be stated again. With GMROI, lowering inventory appears to be just as good as increasing gross margin. If these actions were equally strong, then either would be appropriate. However, they are decidedly different in their financial strength.

Assuming the reader did not nod off while looking at Exhibits 3 and 6, it should be abundantly clear these CPVs are not even close to equal potency. An inventory reduction, as a financial lever, is an 80-pound weakling having sand kicked in its face at the beach. Gross margin is an 800-pound gorilla about to carry Fay Wray off into the night. The difference in the relative strength of these two prongs of the GMROI tool is critical.

In summary, GMROI leads distributors away from the profitability promised land. It is diametrically opposed to managing the firm based on CPV performance. If firms are going to improve profitability, they must evaluate potential trade-offs properly.

GMROI is but one of the multitude of metrics used to evaluate performance for all, or part of, a distribution business. While it is worse than most, the underlying problems associated with GMROI exist in a multitude of other metrics, ranging from sales per employee to the bad-debt loss ratio.

In analyzing performance, firms need to look at as many aspects of a decision as they can (such as the profitability of a product line). They also need to understand and utilize the CPV trade-off process properly.

Moving Forward to Chapter Three

Individual managers may love the hierarchy of CPVs presented here or they may hate it. That love/hate relationship is immaterial. All that is required for success is for managers to understand the hierarchy and employ it properly.

Firms that don't accept the (1) gross margin, (2) expenses, (3) sales volume, and (4) investment hierarchy are more likely to fail the profitability final exam. Firms that don't expand the analysis to consider the trade-offs between the CPVs move from "likely to fail" to "doomed to fail." Firms that use metrics that distort the CPV trade-offs, such as GMROI, deserve to fail.

The next chapter will start the process of looking at the specific actions that can be taken to utilize the CPVs effectively. It will do so by providing a two-for-one bonus. It will look at sales and expenses simultaneously.

Talking Points from Chapter Two

- Distribution companies that try to get around the CPVs are essentially waving a red cape at a bull. They do so at great risk to their financial health.
- The CPV priorities for almost every distributor should be:
  1. Increase the gross margin percentage
  2. Get control of the expenses, especially payroll

3. Plan for reasonable sales growth

4. Monitor—but don't necessarily lower—the investment factors

- Profitability is always about trade-offs. No firm can maximize all of the CPVs simultaneously.

- CPV trade-offs must be based upon financial realities, not the ever-popular conventional wisdom.

3   Sales Myopia

Sales solves all problems. Actually, sales solves most problems. Wait, make that sales solves some problems. What the heck, sales solves some problems and creates some others.

Sales volume would appear to be a relatively easy concept to understand. Lots of sales is a good thing, no sales is a very bad one. However, in the quest for sales all sorts of things get in the way of making sales *profitably*. The challenge for distributors is to understand how sales volume and sales growth really impact their businesses.

The sales discussion is organized into four sections:

- **Sales versus Expenses**—It is not the amount of sales or the rate of sales growth that is the profit issue. It is the cost of generating the sales. Distributors must begin to link sales and expenses more directly.
- **The Sales to Payroll Wedge**—Because of the importance of payroll in the expense mix, firms need to control payroll expenses so that they don't increase as fast as sales. This is what is commonly called a sales to payroll wedge or gap.
- **Making the Wedge a Reality**—In order to make the sales to payroll wedge a reality it is necessary to examine how the firm can modify what is called order economics.
- **Excessive Sales Growth**—It is possible for sales growth to get out of hand. In many cases growth that is too rapid is worse than growth that is too slow.

As with most profitability issues, sales analysis is a complicated concept. That means it is a long chapter, with a fair number of exhibits. In structure the chapter is akin to eating an artichoke. It is necessary to get through some of the bitter outer leaves before the juicy inner ones can be savored.

With yet another pained analogy in print, read on.

Sales versus Expenses

To understand the sales issue requires retreating back to Chapter Two for two brief reminders. Reminder #1 is that the slope of the graph for expense reductions in relationship to ROA (Exhibit 5) was actually steeper than the slope of the graph for sales increases (Exhibit 4). Reminder #2 is that for distributors expenses are heavily weighted towards payroll (Exhibit 2).

The implication from Reminder #1 is that sales and expenses must be viewed in unison. In simplest terms, profit will increase if expenses can be controlled so that they rise less than sales, while profit will not increase if expenses rise faster than sales. Sales growth and expenses are two halves of the same profit canoe. Yet another terrible metaphor added to the list.

The implication of Reminder #2 is that the name of the game in expenses is payroll. It is not that other expenses will take care of themselves. It is that they will *kind of* take care of themselves.

As sales increase over time there are more deliveries to be made, more invoices to process and the like. More staffing is required. The result is higher payroll. In contrast, a lot of non-payroll expenses can be leveraged as the firm increases its sales. That is, many (but not all) non-payroll expenses rise more in relationship to inflation than in relationship to sales.

Payroll tends to be highly related to sales plus it has the additional kicker of increasing with inflation. Because of the sheer size of payroll and its tendency to increase relentlessly, it must be given top priority. If payroll is not controlled it pretty much will not matter what happens to the other expenses.

The Lack of Progress

The historical track record with regard to payroll control is not encouraging. To be less subtle, it is very disturbing. This can be seen in **Exhibit 9** which presents information on payroll expenses as a percent of sales for the distribution industries tracked by The Profit Planning Group. [11]

The graph indicates that there have been ups and downs, but nothing has really happened. The ability to make improvements in payroll as a percent of sales has been nonexistent. To a certain extent this is reminiscent of good old Exhibit 1 which suggested that not a lot has happened over the years with regard to ROA in distribution.

---

[11] The Profit Planning Group, as stated in Chapter One, has information for more than 40 lines of trade going back more than 30 years in some instances. While Exhibit 9 is for a single line of trade, it represents a pattern that is duplicated in almost every line of trade.

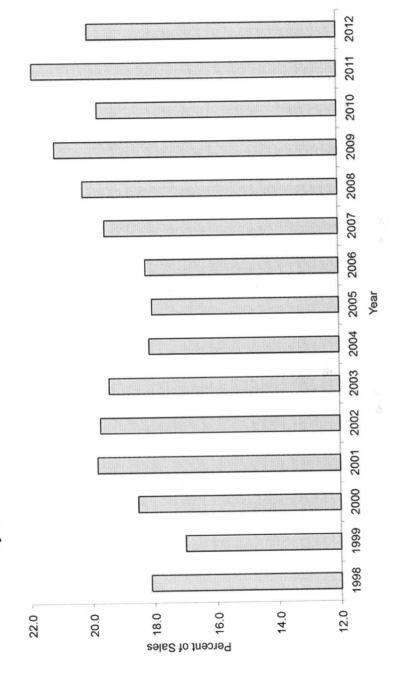

Exhibit 9
Payroll as a Percent of Sales for a Specific Distribution Line of Trade

The lack of improvement demonstrated over the last 10–20 years means that sales and payroll essentially have grown at the same rate. Some years sales grows faster than payroll; in other years the relationship is reversed.

This lack of a sustained improvement in payroll is a little surprising given the rather consistent investment in productivity-enhancing technology made by distributors in aggregate. A few of the innovations (some of which the author doesn't begin to understand) include:

- Bar Coding
- Fleet Scheduling
- Activity-Based Costing
- Internet Sales
- Supply Chain Management
- RFID Technology

To get professorial for a brief moment, an investment in improved systems and procedures is a necessary, but not sufficient, action for controlling payroll costs. Without improved systems firms lag behind. With systems, they merely stay in place. This "necessary, but not sufficient" issue needs to be understood.

Necessary—If investments in technology are not made, payroll costs will not stay steady as a percent of sales. They will increase; eventually to the point the firm cannot be competitive.

The classic real-world manifestation of this can be seen by stepping away from wholesale distribution for a moment and looking at the competitive battles between Walmart and Kmart in retailing during the early part of this century. While numerous factors went into the differences in fortunes between the two firms, the investment in technology was one of the major ones.

Walmart invested heavily in technology during the latter part of the twentieth century and first part of the twenty-first. Kmart did not. As a result, Walmart dramatically enhanced its operating advantage over Kmart. Even if the two firms had been equal in everything else, Walmart would still have had a cost advantage that simply could not be overcome.

Sufficient—Systems and procedures, by themselves, do not guarantee that payroll costs will decline. About the best they can do is help the firm stay equal to other, well-managed, firms making similar system improvements.

Non-system factors are what need to be addressed in greater detail. For example, the habit of automatic pay raises for employees each year is a serious issue. Too many firms pay employees for breathing. The employees who have breathed the longest in the firm get paid the most. Until this is changed, payroll costs will not be controlled.

In addition, many distributors have aggressively expanded their service profile. Additional services, by definition, require additional personnel to provide those services. Some service enhancements have been strategic in nature. A few others have done little more than increase payroll.

The most serious issue though, is that management has not utilized a planning metric for dealing with payroll. It also does not have proper mechanisms for putting such metrics into place. Time to deal with both issues.

The Sales to Payroll Wedge

The key to getting payroll under control is something called the Sales to Payroll Wedge. The wedge has two components.

Sales Growth—Sales must grow by at least the inflation rate plus some safety factor. A reasonable safety factor is 3.0%. Over the last dozen years or so the compound annual growth rate for inflation has checked in at almost exactly 2.0% (2.04% actually). Adding a 3.0% safety factor comes to a *minimum* sales growth rate of 5.0%. There is no maximum growth rate. At least not yet.

In 1980, as a historical note, the inflation rate was 13.5%. This remains the indoor track record for the United States. A return to those halcyon days would require sales growth of 16.5% (13.5% plus 3.0%). Whatever the inflation rate, the 3.0% safety factor remains.

As a reminder, the 5.0% growth mandate (using current inflation levels) is the minimum. There is no maximum. Later in this chapter it will be suggested that torrid sales growth is as bad as pallid growth. For now, sales growth must be somewhere between 5.0% and infinity.

Payroll Growth—Fully-loaded payroll must grow 2.0% less than sales grows. This difference in growth rates is the essence of the sales to payroll wedge. With the aforementioned 5.0% sales growth, payroll can only be allowed to increase by 3.0%.

The casual reader may conclude that these are two easy hurdles to clear. The casual reader would be well served to look at Exhibit 9 once again. If improvements in payroll as a percent of sales have been a mirage in recent history, it will be difficult to make them solid in the future.

Sales to Payroll Wedge Alternatives

Despite the outstanding quality of the discussion in the previous section, many readers still believe that rapid sales growth will overcome all problems. Time to take a look and see.

Exhibit 10 examines two very different sales growth scenarios for the omnipresent Mountain View. One scenario explores 5.0% sales growth which would reflect a mature industry, like most of distribution. The second scenario provides a glimpse at 15.0% sales growth, often called nirvana.

Exhibit 10
The Profit Impact of a Sales to Payroll Wedge
Mountain View Distributing, Inc.

Income Statement ($)	Current Results	2.0% Sales to Payroll Wedge 5.0% Sales Growth	15.0% Sales Growth
Net Sales	$20,000,000	$21,000,000	$23,000,000
Cost of Goods Sold	15,000,000	15,750,000	17,250,000
Gross Margin	5,000,000	5,250,000	5,750,000
Expenses			
Payroll and Fringe Benefits	3,000,000	3,090,000	3,390,000
All Other Expenses	1,500,000	1,575,000	1,725,000
Total Expenses	4,500,000	4,665,000	5,115,000
Profit Before Taxes	$500,000	$585,000	$635,000
Income Statement (%)			
Net Sales	100.0	100.0	100.0
Cost of Goods Sold	75.0	75.0	75.0
Gross Margin	25.0	25.0	25.0
Expenses			
Payroll and Fringe Benefits	15.0	14.7	14.7
All Other Expenses	7.5	7.5	7.5
Total Expenses	22.5	22.2	22.2
Profit Before Taxes	2.5	2.8	2.8

The first column of numbers merely replicates Mountain View's current financial situation as first presented in Exhibit 2. As a reminder, $20.0 million in sales, a gross margin of 25.0% of sales and a pre-tax profit of 2.5% of sales. Total expenses are heavily weighted towards payroll and fringe benefits.

The last two columns examine the impact of the sales to payroll wedge under the two growth assumptions presented before—5.0% and 15.0%. In another burst of creativity the author has labeled them 5.0% Sales Growth and 15.0% Sales Growth. The same logic applies to both of them.

Slow Growth—In the 5.0% growth column sales have grown by, not surprisingly, 5.0%. This growth was achieved with no change in the gross margin percentage. As a result, both cost of goods sold and gross margin also increase by 5.0%.

The real impact in this column is that payroll expense only increases by 3.0%. This provides for the mathematical reality of a 2.0% sales to payroll wedge (5.0% sales growth minus 3.0% payroll growth for the arithmetically challenged).

The other expenses (all of those non-payroll necessities like rent, utilities, interest and the like) are assumed to increase at the same rate as sales. On the continuum of good to bad assumptions, this ranks as one of the worst of all times.

As sales increase, it should be possible to "leverage" the other expenses. That is, they should probably not increase as quickly as sales. Since there is no expense leveraging here (sales and all other expenses are growing at the same rate), the exhibit demonstrates the impact of the sales to payroll wedge *in and of itself*. The exhibit isolates the impact of this single action. The lousy assumption makes for good analysis.

As can be seen, the very modest 5.0% sales growth does wonders for the bottom line if the sales to payroll wedge can be implemented. Profit increases from $500,000 to $585,000, an increase of 17.0%. A glance at the bottom of the column indicates that profit is now 2.8% of sales.

The .3 percentage point bump in profit comes from a .3 percentage point decline in payroll as a percent of sales. A metric (payroll as a percent of sales) that hasn't gone down in 15 years is now heading south systematically.

Fast Growth—The last column examines the impact of more rapid growth, defined here as a 15.0% increase in sales. The same sorts of impacts that were seen in the 5.0% column are also at work here. The gross margin percentage stays at 25.0%, so sales, cost of goods and gross margin all increase by 15.0%.

The 2.0% sales to payroll wedge steps forward majestically at this point so payroll only increases by 13.0%. The other expenses follow the same growth path as sales and increase by 15.0%. The same poor assumption, but the same ability to isolate only the impact of the sales to payroll wedge.

The end result is that profit increases by 27.0% to $635,000. The profit margin ends up at 2.8% which was the same as for the 5.0% increase in sales.

Astute readers (which includes all three of the people who actually buy this book) will note that a profit of $635,000 is more than $585,000. It appears that Dr. Finance Man doesn't know what he is talking about. That is not only possible, but very likely. However…

To get to $635,000 in profit versus $585,000, the firm had to generate another $2.0 million in sales and probably *hire more employees* as payroll increased to $3.39 million. It was a lot more work, for not a whole lot more profit. While more is more, whether the effort was worth it can be called into question.

Time for the punch line. Sales growth by itself doesn't mean doodly-squat (pardon the technical term). Profit can be increased substantially with any sales growth rate north of 5.0% (actually north of inflation plus 3.0%). The only thing that really matters is how much sales can be increased *in relationship to how much payroll has to increase* to support that sales growth.

Pushing the Sales to Payroll Wedge Envelope

The fact that sales growth and payroll growth must be examined together is an absolutely essential concept for distributors to understand. The concept must be combined with the reality that a 2.0% sales to payroll wedge is absolutely truckin'. Anything beyond that is outside the realm of possibility.

The fact that it is impossible doesn't stop distributors from charging ahead into areas of performance that can't be reached. For example, management may decide that sales are going to grow by 15.0%. Since a 2.0% sales to payroll wedge is good, then a 12.0% wedge must be great. So, a plan is born, sales will grow by 15.0% and payroll will only grow by 3.0% to produce a 12.0% sales to payroll wedge. Your favorite author will do the math; profit would increase to $935,000.

There is one minor problem with this daydream: It doesn't work. If this is too subtle, review Exhibit 9 once again. Payroll as a percent of sales really hasn't changed in distribution over the course of the last twenty years. Ergo, producing even a 2.0% sales to payroll wedge will be a major achievement. Don't get greedy in planning.

In point of fact, a meager 1.0% sales to payroll wedge would still put more on the bottom line. This can be seen in **Exhibit 11** which looks at a lot of permutations in the sales to payroll wedge. All of the permutations revolve around the assumption that sales will increase by 5.0%.

Accompanying the 5.0% sales growth is an increase in payroll expense ranging from 1.0% to 9.0%. That produces a series of sales to payroll wedges ranging from 4.0% to -4.0%. In must be noted yet again that for each of the rows sales has increased by the same 5.0%, to $21.0 million.

If payroll increases by only 1.0% (the technical term for this is *impossible*), then profit explodes from the current $500,000 to $645,000, an increase of 29.0%. At the other extreme, if the firm has to make infrastructure investments (a euphemism for expenses getting out of control) so that payroll increases by 9.0%, then profit actually declines.

Exhibit 11
The Impact on Profit of Decreasing Levels of
a Sales to Payroll Wedge
Mountain View Distributing, Inc.

Sales Growth (%)	Payroll Growth (%)	Sales to Payroll Wedge (%)	Profit	Profit Growth (%)
5.0	1.0	4.0	$645,000	29.0
5.0	2.0	3.0	615,000	23.0
5.0	3.0	2.0	585,000	17.0
5.0	4.0	1.0	555,000	11.0
5.0	5.0	0.0	525,000	5.0
5.0	6.0	-1.0	495,000	-1.0
5.0	7.0	-2.0	465,000	-7.0
5.0	8.0	-3.0	435,000	-13.0
5.0	9.0	-4.0	405,000	-19.0

It is useful to check out the middle row with 5.0% payroll growth. Sales and payroll are now increasing at the same exact rate—the historical long-term reality. Profit increases by a somnambulistic 5.0%. It is the reason the payroll percentage has never decreased. One year there is a slightly positive wedge, the next year a slightly negative one. After ten years, the firm ends up right back where it started. Larger, of course, but not a lot more profitable as profit has only increased as fast as sales.

Making the Wedge a Reality

At this point, producing a sales growth to payroll growth wedge should seem like a great idea. Although readers can quibble with the 2.0% figure if they desire, a wedge of some size seems essential. The issue now is to identify how such a wedge can be generated.

This is where your scrivener's true brilliance shows through: Stop doing so many things that are bad for you and start doing more of the things that are good for you. The secret is to know which are which.

The things that are bad for you almost always revolve around wanting what the firm does not now have. Namely, the firm wants to grab customers that are not already buying from it and convince them to buy. It is something that really should be done, but in moderation. Kind of like tattoos.

Making the assumption that potential customers are free to buy from whatever firm they desire, there is a reason some don't buy from your wonderful company. They blooming don't want to.

Almost every salesperson in distribution has heard a potential customer say something like: "My grandfather bought from your company in 1978 and your sales rep was rude. We haven't bought from you since and we sure aren't going to start now. Thanks for coming by."

Everybody has seen a restaurant with a giant sign in the window: *Under New Management.* What that sign really means is *Not As Bad As We Used To Be.* It is a plaintive effort to distance themselves from the past.

Luckily, not every non-buying potential customer hates your firm. However, a full 100.0% of them do prefer to buy from another firm. Trying to convert them is something that must be done. However, be prepared for a long, hard slog.

Things That are Good for You #1

Luckily there are a lot of customers who like to buy from you. Some of them buy a little, some buy a lot; they all buy something. The key is to work with these customers to get them to (a) buy more, and (b) buy in a way that generates a higher level of profit for you.

A quick reminder: The goal is not simply to increase sales. The goal is to increase sales *more* than payroll must increase to support the higher sales. This gets into the realm of order economics.

Simply put, order economics involves the composition of orders. Three things are crucial here: (1) the number of lines on every order, (2) the fill rate (or service level) on those order lines, and (3) the average line value. In plain English, use these three tools to get customers to buy more every time they order.

From a sales to payroll wedge perspective there is a hierarchy associated with these three factors: the fill rate is most important, the average line value is second and the lines per order is third. They are all important. Just as with the CPVs themselves, though, some are just more important than others.

Nobody noticed at the time, but in Exhibit 2 it was mentioned that the firm has an average order value of $500. This is pretty close to reality for a lot of firms in distribution. It doesn't make a lot of difference if it is $500, $50 or $5,000. It is simply a starting point.

If the firm is generating $20.0 million in sales and doing it $500 at a time, then it must be processing 40,000 orders per year ($20,000,000 divided by $500). This is a lot of work and a tribute to how productive distributors really are.

In point of fact, distributors are off-the-chart productive. They are able to process a huge number of small orders and still be profitable. It is remarkable operating performance. The accolades won't last long, though.

Exhibit 12 uses the 40,000 orders as a jumping off point. In the Current column that is the number of orders generated. It stays the same in the Potential column. That is, the firm is not going after any new customers. Of course, it should go after new customers. What the exhibit focuses on is how to drive the sales to payroll wedge from *existing* customers.

Lines per Order—The second row in the exhibit introduces a new measurement, namely the number of lines on every order. That is, it is the number of *different* items being ordered. In the Current column this is assumed to be an average of 3.5 lines per order. Again, not that far removed from a lot of firms in distribution. In the Potential column this number explodes to 3.6. Make a mental note that this sure isn't very much of an improvement.

Driving the lines per order to a higher level involves two actions. The first is to have the sales force do more add-on selling. You mean, have the sales force actually do its job? Well, yes that does come to mind.

The problem with add-on sales is that salespeople are humans (the root of all problems, incidentally). They get tired of being told no when they attempt add-on selling. What the exhibit says is that they should overcome this issue and strive for add-on sales every time. On nine straight orders they are told no. Then the clouds part and on the tenth order they add one more line to the order. It may seem puny, but it really starts to add up.

Exhibit 12
The Sales Impact of Order Economics
Mountain View Distributing, Inc.

	Item		Current	Potential
1	Number of Orders		40,000	40,000
2	Lines per Order		3.5	3.6
3	Lines Ordered	[1 x 2]	140,000	144,000
4	Fill Rate		95.2%	95.3%
5	Lines Filled	[3 x 4]	133,333	137,232
6	Average Order Line		$150.00	$151.50
7	Net Sales	[5 x 6]	$20,000,000	$20,790,648

The key to making this a reality is measurement. If the firm has no idea how many lines are on the typical order, it has no chance of improving it. This gets back into the realm of implementing better systems.

The second action in driving more lines per order is to ensure that customers are aware of everything in the firm's assortment. Nothing wrong with telling them over and over about one-stop shopping.

Putting more lines on every order causes payroll expenses to go up just a smidgen as there are now 144,000 *potential* order lines to fill rather than the 140,000 originally (Line 3). More things will have to be pulled off the shelf in the warehouse and more things will have to be put on and taken off of trucks. However, the payroll increase is really small (actually a smidgen).

Fill Rate—A few paragraphs ago it was suggested that the fill rate is the most important of the three drivers of the sales to payroll wedge. This is because if you don't have it you can't sell it, and if you don't have it often enough, all of your customers go away. Then you have to make a lot of changes and hang out your *Not As Bad As We Used To Be* sign. It is a lot easier to chase customers off than it is to get them back.

A fairly common rule of thumb in distribution is to shoot for a 95.0% fill rate. Some firms do much better than this, some do demonstrably worse. Mountain View is in the 95.0% mold, but actually does just slightly better with a 95.2% fill rate. The purchasing department gets a small accolade.

Once again, the target improvement to be made is tiny. The fill rate moves from 95.2% to 95.3%. The net effect is that there are now 137,323 lines filled versus the 133,333 before (Line 5 on Exhibit 12).

Some readers (call them CFOs) will complain (or maybe even whine) that increasing the fill rate will require the firm to carry more inventory and that this is the kiss of death to profitability. At this point such readers must go back to Exhibits 4 and 6 for a remedial course. The sales graph (Exhibit 4) was relatively steep while the inventory graph (Exhibit 6) was flatter than an Academy Awards show.

Adding inventory to support an increase in sales is *always* a good idea. Of course, adding inventory without increasing sales is a terrible idea. The reality is that way too many firms have repeatedly cut inventory to the point that sales are impacted negatively. To coin a brilliant phrase never heard before: "Can't sell apples from an empty cart."

Average Line Value—This is the second most important driver in improving order economics. It is by far the most difficult to influence. At least it appears to be. However, there is still hope.

The least difficult (nothing is ever easy) way to increase this value is to raise prices. That discussion will be deferred to the next chapter. For now, simply note it is a very serious option that can't be ignored.

The second approach is to make use of the "good, better, best" concept. Every product line has variants that can be massaged by an effective sales force.

Finally, customers could be encouraged to order more product at a time. That is, instead of buying one case, they will buy two. This seemingly defies logic as customers order the quantity they think they need. Don't you just hate them!

In actuality, most customers order hand to mouth and place way too many orders. They actually increase their own costs by ordering too frequently. The author will reluctantly admit defeat on this one. It is blooming hard to convince them to place fewer, but larger, orders. Still important to try though.

At long last, Exhibit 12 reaches its crescendo. If the average line value is increased from $150.00 to $151.50, it has gone up by a staggering 1.0%. It may be small, but it was achieved without any increase in order picking, etc. There were more commissions paid, but it drives a huge sales to payroll wedge.

The overall result in Exhibit 12 is that sales increased through improved order economics from $20.0 million to almost $20.8 million. The increase is just short of 4.0% and has almost no impact on payroll. If the firm can add to this a little inflation, normal market growth and the occasional new account, sales growth should end up well in excess of 5.0%. It should also result in a nice sales to payroll wedge.

Running and Hiding—In Chapter One it was suggested that firms not only had to deal with operational factors to be best of breed. They also had to have a market position that allowed them to run and hide from competition. It may not seem like it at first glance, but getting control over order economics is actually a form of running and hiding.

When firms troll for new customers, reduce prices or open new branches, their actions are known to the world. In contrast, improving the fill rate, putting an extra line on an order every once in a while and pushing a good, better, best mentality is virtually invisible to the competition. The running and hiding was not accomplished by a great strategic breakthrough. It was done by doing things that competitors don't really realize are all that important.

To a certain extent this is somewhat like having a barrier to entry. That barrier is actually having a system to measure and control the key factors in order economics. It is not as good as outlawing competition, but is still nice.

Things That are Good for You #2

The previous section made the necessary mathematical assumption that one order is pretty much like another. Of course, during the course of the year some orders are for $25,000 and some are for $0.89. The economics are slightly different.

Such differences accumulate when the analysis is carried beyond individual orders to the specific customers that are generating those orders. Some customers order a lot at a time, some order much less. Some customers generate a lot of returns (which are never their fault, incidentally) while some have very few. Some customers have a lot of emergency orders, others have very few. Some customers tie up the time of the sales force, others do not. Ad infinitum.

As it turns out, some customers are good for distributors with respect to many of the issues cited in the previous paragraph. As a result, they tend to be highly profitable for the distributor to serve. At the other end of the inevitable spectrum, some customers are terrible. It really helps to know which are which. [12]

Exhibit 13 summarizes the profit impact of different customer groups. It is a set of relationships that pops up every time such an analysis is conducted, regardless of the line of trade. In the exhibit customers are assigned to four groups—A, B, C and D. One again creativity bedazzles the reader.

Exhibit 13
The Sales and Profit Profile of Different Customer Groups
Mountain View Distributing, Inc.

Customer Profit Category	Percent of Customers	Number of Customers	Percent of Profit	Profit	Profit per Customer
A	15.0	150	100.0	$500,000	$3,333
B	15.0	150	35.0	175,000	1,167
C	35.0	350	10.0	50,000	143
D	35.0	350	-45.0	-225,000	-643
	100.0	1,000	100.0	$500,000	$500

---

[12] Figuring out which are which requires technical skills that are far beyond the analytical capabilities of the author. For insights into the process, see Brent Gover, *In Search of the Perfect Customer: Cost-to-Serve for Distributors,* National Association of Wholesaler-Distributors, 2011.

The first thing to note is that the four Customer Profit Groups (A through D) are not based upon how much the customer purchases. Instead, the hierarchy is built upon on how profitable they are to the distributor.

Let's assume Mountain View has 1,000 customers. Of these, about 150 generate a *lot* of profit for the firm. A lot is defined here as all of it. That is, the firm makes the equivalent of its total profit ($500,000) from only 15.0% of its customers.

Theoretically, the firm could eliminate all of its other customers, only work a couple of days a week and still make $500,000. That thought is, indeed, very theoretical. There are a lot of reasons to have other customers, such as helping the firm buy better, covering some overhead expenses and the like. Even so, 100.0% is still 100.0%.

Interestingly, the firm also generates a profit on the B and C accounts. In total, the A, B and C accounts produce a profit of $725,000. The D accounts pile up a loss of $225,000. Stated somewhat differently, the firm likes the D accounts so much it is willing to sacrifice $225,000 in profit for the thrill of servicing them.

At this point the temptation to bring out the meat axe gets even stronger. Surely, the D accounts could be slashed without harm. That may well be correct, but it is still a little strong. There are really two distinct types of D accounts.

There is a small group of *Unprofitable and Proud of It* D accounts. In most firms this is about 2.0% of the total customer count. For Mountain View, that 2.0% would be somewhere in the general vicinity of 20 customers. These can be bid adieu with a clean conscience.

Even here there is a note of caution. It is probably not a good idea to tell these customers, "You know, I have never liked you. By the way your spouse is ugly and your dog can't hunt." This tends to generate bad karma that surfaces again next year when this customer acquires your most profitable account.

A much better way is to allow these problem customers to fire themselves. The appropriate strategy is to just keep raising prices to these accounts until they decide it might be better to concentrate all of their unprofitable purchases with your competitor.

After 20 customers are sent to the showers, there are still 320 accounts that buy in a way that doesn't generate any profit. This represents a lot of customers to work with in order to change the order economic issues that were discussed before. It should be a slow, methodical process.

Even if the only result of working with the unprofitable 320 is to make them a little less unprofitable, that is an improvement. By continually emphasizing order economics a lot of small improvements can be generated. In aggregate the small improvements eventually become a large one.

Excessive Sales Growth

So far, this chapter has built a strong (the author's mother would say brilliant) case for generating profit by driving a wedge between sales growth and payroll growth. The argument was made that 5.0% growth is just as good as 15.0% growth given the necessity for controlling payroll.

At the same time, some folks (yes, Sales Managers once again) would respond that the author should get a life. Rapid sales growth builds enthusism and creates a company poised to dominate the future. To say nothing of generating bonuses for Sales Managers.

As it turns out, rapid growth creates as many problems as it solves. One of those problems is that the firm will probably die. That would appear to be an important enough issue to warrant further discussion.

The further discussion necessitates looking at the world's ugliest formula. It is called the Growth Potential Index (GPI) and is resting comfortably in **Exhibit 14**. The GPI provides an *estimate* of how fast the firm can grow without using up its precious cash reserves, which are only $125,000 (Exhibit 2). At this point it is best to do the calculation and then figure out its implications.

Exhibit 14
The Growth Potential Index
Mountain View Distributing, Inc.

$$\frac{\text{Cash Coming In}}{\text{What Cash is Needed for}}$$

$$=$$

$$\frac{\text{Profit (After Taxes)}}{\text{Inventory + Accounts Receivable - Accounts Payable}}$$

$$=$$

$$\frac{\$350,000}{\$2,500,000 \ + \ \$2,187,500 \ - \ \$1,000,000}$$

$$=$$

$$\frac{\$350,000}{\$3,687,500}$$

$$=$$

$$9.5\%$$

The formula relates the cash coming into the business to the cash that will be needed to finance growth. The numerator defines cash coming in as the profit that the firm generates, but now on an *after-tax* basis. The firm generated $500,000 in pre-tax profit. With a 30.0% tax rate this provides for $350,000 after taxes. If this doesn't cover the needed investment for growth, then the firm will use up some of its cash.

The denominator reflects what cash is needed for. There are two investment categories that will rise along with sales. Inventory will more or less increase with sales over time. Accounts receivable will automatically increase with sales on a real-time basis. Offsetting these investments is the fact that as the firm grows it will purchase more and have more accounts payable to offset the need for additional cash. All of the items in the denominator come from Exhibit 2.

For Mountain View the GPI is 9.5%. The calculation is straightforward enough, although the math is a little dicey. The implication is much less so. It is also blatantly contrary to all logic.

Sales Growth, Profit and Cash—If the firm grows faster than 9.5% it should (let's assume it actually will) generate more profit on the higher sales. It would seem logical that the firm would have more cash. Let's use 15.0% sales growth as an example.

Sales growth of 15.0% will cause the firm to have to invest 15.0% more in inventory and accounts receivable. This will be offset by 15.0% more in accounts payable. At this point the firm is investing to support growth faster than cash is coming in. The faster it grows the more it will need an ever-increasing investment to support higher sales. Cash will actually fall. Don't object yet, a proof is on the way.

If the firm grows slower than 9.5% it will actually bring in more cash than it needs for expansion and cash reserves will build up. At the same time, though, with the lower level of sales it will have less profit.

For sales growth, the faster the growth the higher the profit, but the lower the cash. Lesser of two evils? Rock and a hard place? Grow fast, make a lot of profit, but run out of cash. Grow slow, don't make much profit but have cash. This conundrum will be resolved in Chapter Six. For now, a more fundamental issue is on the table. Is that GPI stuff really right? Come on man, more profit and less cash?

Driving More Rapid Sales Growth

Exhibit 15 examines the situation in which Mountain View's management team tells the author to stick the old GPI in his gin and tonic and drink it.

The firm is going to grow by 15.0% and love it. Management closes the sales meeting with a rousing rendition of that ancient rock and roll standard, *I Don't Care What People Say, Rapid Growth Is Here To Stay.*[13]

To nobody's surprise by now, the first column of numbers shows where the firm is currently. It includes both an income statement and a partial balance sheet. The second column details what 15.0% sales growth does for (or to) the firm. There is a lot going on in the exhibit. It will be necessary to skip around, so follow the bouncing ball closely.

Exhibit 15
The Impact of 15.0% Sales Growth
Combined with a Profit Improvement Plan
Mountain View Distributing, Inc.

Income Statement	Current Results	15.0% Growth	Percent Change
Net Sales	$20,000,000	$23,000,000	15.0
Cost of Goods Sold	15,000,000	17,250,000	15.0
Gross Margin	5,000,000	5,750,000	15.0
Expenses			
Payroll and Fringe Benefits	3,000,000	3,390,000	13.0
All Other Expenses	1,500,000	1,695,000	13.0
Total Expenses	4,500,000	5,085,000	13.0
Profit Before Taxes	500,000	665,000	33.0
Income Taxes (30.0% of PBT)	150,000	199,500	33.0
Profit After Taxes	$350,000	$465,500	33.0
Partial Balance Sheet			
Cash	$125,000	-$112,625	-190.1
Accounts Receivable	2,187,500	2,515,625	15.0
Inventory	2,500,000	2,875,000	15.0
Other Current Assets	62,500	62,500	0.0
Total Current Assets	4,875,000	5,340,500	9.5
Fixed Assets	1,375,000	1,375,000	0.0
Total Assets	$6,250,000	$6,715,500	7.4

The income statement is relatively direct. The firm has increased its sales by 15.0% while keeping the gross margin percentage the same. It has driven a 2.0% wedge between sales growth and payroll growth. In addition, it has leveraged the other expenses so they also increase 2.0% less than sales. It has moved beyond the simple sales to payroll wedge. It now has a sales to total expenses wedge. Even more profit!

---

[13] For readers under the age of 70, *Rock and Roll Is Here To Stay* was recorded by Danny & The Juniors in 1958. Coincidentally, this was the last year in which the author had an original thought.

The bottom of the income statement shows the payoff from this. Pre-tax profit goes to $665,000. After the obligatory income taxes (still a 30% rate), the after-tax profit is $465,500.

It is now time to jump to the very bottom of the balance sheet. In the 15.0% Growth column, total assets have been increased by the amount of the after-tax profit of $465,500. That is, every single penny of profit that the firm generates is reinvested back into the business. No vacation home, no new boat. Everything is plowed back into the business. This means that total assets are now $6,715,500.

Working from the bottom of the balance sheet to the top, it is assumed that fixed assets stay the same. No new car either. Therefore total current assets have increased by the amount of the after-tax profit reinvestment.

Continuing to work from the bottom to the top, other current assets are an insignificant $62,500. Probably don't need any more prepaid expenses, so ignore this as it only gets in the way.

Now for the coup de grâce to those sales managers wanting fast growth. Both inventory and accounts receivable have increased by 15.0% to support the increase in sales. For inventory this is what will happen inevitably, albeit eventually. For accounts receivable this is what will happen automatically and instantly.

Cash has to be what is left over after working all the way up from the bottom. It is a very comfortable -$112,625. Yes, that is a minus sign. The company was highly profitable right up until the day it died.[14]

Stop grinding your teeth. Of course, the firm could have used up more of its line of credit to offset the cash drain—assuming the bank really wants to lend to a firm with lousy cash flow. Also one final note, when times get bad, the firms with lots of debt go out of business first.

In short, firms would be much better served to generate a nice hunk of profit, but do so while growing at a more moderate rate. The firm will have to forego the psychic income associated with rapid growth; however, it would be both highly profitable and financially strong. Not a bad combination.

The author can rest comfortably at night knowing that not a single reader of this book is going to commit to growing at a moderate rate. New business simply cannot be turned away. On top of that, the Sales Manager is your son and he really needs that bonus for driving more sales.

---

[14] A quick technical note. If the firm had grown at 9.5% (its GPI) and leveraged total expenses by the same 2.0% wedge, it would have ended up with cash of $125,938, virtually right back where it started. Neat, huh?

Having said that, firms should think carefully about how rapid sales growth can be leveraged properly. They should also give extremely careful thought to cash flow. Unfortunately, thinking about cash flow may lead to some really bizarre decisions. That discussion will have to be held until Chapter Six. In the meantime, sales growth must lead to profit growth.

Moving Forward to Chapter Four

Sales volume is everybody's favorite CPV. Increasing sales means that the firm is dynamic and vibrant. It is the raison d'être for the entire firm. Nothing happens until somebody sells something is still a truism.

At the same time, sales without an accompanying dose of expense control is always an exercise in getting larger but never getting better. If the expense control comes in the form of managing order economics, then the impact of sales on profit is dramatic.

The large fly in the soup is that the quest for sales growth (if left unchecked) will inevitably lead to a collapse of pricing integrity. Gross margin, which was identified as the most important CPV, must be brought into the profit equation along with sales and expenses.

PowerPoint® Bullets from Chapter Three

- Some reasonable level of sales growth is essential for success. At a minimum, sales must grow by at least the rate of inflation plus 3.0%.
- Making sales growth actually produce profits requires simultaneously controlling payroll so that it grows 2.0% slower than sales (sales to payroll wedge).
- Non-payroll expenses can be given benign neglect. Over time with consistent sales growth they should decline modestly as a percent of sales.
- Moderate sales growth is just as good as rapid sales growth as long as expenses are controlled.
- Getting control of payroll requires a strong focus on order economics in order to produce small improvements over time.
- Bad order economics are generally concentrated in problem customers who end up in the D customer group.
- Excessive sales growth creates serious cash flow problems. Growth expectations should be tempered to reflect this reality.

4 Gross Margin Defeatism

To a real extent, gross margin is something like Gulliver in his travels among the Lilliputians. Gross margin is the single most important determinant of profit. At the same time, it is the most difficult factor for distributors to improve. It is exactly like Gulliver being pinned to the earth by those pesky little Lilliputians.

Gross margin is also like Gulliver with regard to the size of this chapter. It weighs in at a behemoth 8,000 words or so, some of them multi-syllabic. Given the importance of gross margin, every word is needed.[15] The discussion will be broken into three topics:

- **Making It Up With Volume**—Almost all of the low-price retail competitors, such as Walmart, also tend to be high-volume ones. This leads to a natural desire to develop a "make it up with volume" profit model. It is not impossible in distribution, but it does require some serious rethinking. The economics of such moves need to be understood.

- **Obliterating the Cost-Plus Mentality**—All pricing decisions in distribution start with cost. Whether a pure cost-plus model is used or a more sophisticated process is employed, it is still a cost-plus mentality. This may be too subtle, but cost-plus is to gross margin improvement what the Black Death was to population growth in medieval Europe. It is something more than a minor issue.

- **Pricing for Profit**—Distributors desperately need a pricing model that provides for higher profit while also providing an effective competitive shield against those wily Internet competitors and big box store operators.

---

[15] By comparison, the Patient Protection and Affordable Care Act contains 425,116 words, none of which are devoted to improving distributor profitability.

Before moving forward with efforts to improve gross margin, it is useful to review just how important it is to profitability. **Exhibit 16** takes the materials presented in three different graphs in Chapter One and combines them into one single graph for comparison purposes. The graph looks at the impact on the firm's bottom line by making improvements in the three most important of the CPVs—sales volume, gross margin and expenses.

Inventory and accounts receivable are not covered in the exhibit as their graphs were extremely flat. These two items have not been consigned to the trash heap of history. They are simply being given benign neglect for a moment. They will return triumphantly in the discussion of cash flow in Chapter Six.

What was true in Chapter One is still true here. Gross margin is represented by the steepest line in Exhibit 16. Given the overwhelming importance of gross margin, it seems logical that distributors would be paranoid about improving it. In practice, most firms give lip service to margin enhancements, but really don't do much at all. The reason is fear.

Eventually, enhancing margin will necessitate some selective price increases. For a lot of distributors, raising prices is considered a dead-end street. De facto, improving margin means raising prices and, as you well know, "That can't be done in an industry as competitive as ours."

While the authors of financial books can belittle such attitudes, they are based upon two very real issues. The first is that the potential for increased price competition is extremely large. The second is that price cutters get great press.

Increased Price Competition—New forms of competition seem to be everywhere. The rise of Internet sales has impacted almost every line of trade. Competitors in other geographic markets can employ the Internet to sell into "our territory" on a low-price basis. In many lines of trade the price issue is complicated by the impact of big box stores selling a wide range of products on a business-to-business basis. These are very legitimate price concerns.

Price Cutter Visibility—It seems like almost all of the success stories ballyhooed in both the business and popular press are about price-driven firms. Amazon, Walmart, Southwest Airlines, Priceline, Scottrade, Geico and a slew of other firms are all touted as role models for competitive strategies. Google, for crying out loud, gives away e-mail and Internet search services. Lower your prices and join the competitive revolution of the twenty-first century.

There is little wonder that distributors are at the point of throwing in the towel on margin improvements, especially if they involve price increases. However, before doing so every distributor should take one more look at Exhibit 16. If gross margin is so important, and it is, then firms should at

Exhibit 16
The Impact of Improving Three CPVs
on Return on Assets
Mountain View Distributing, Inc.

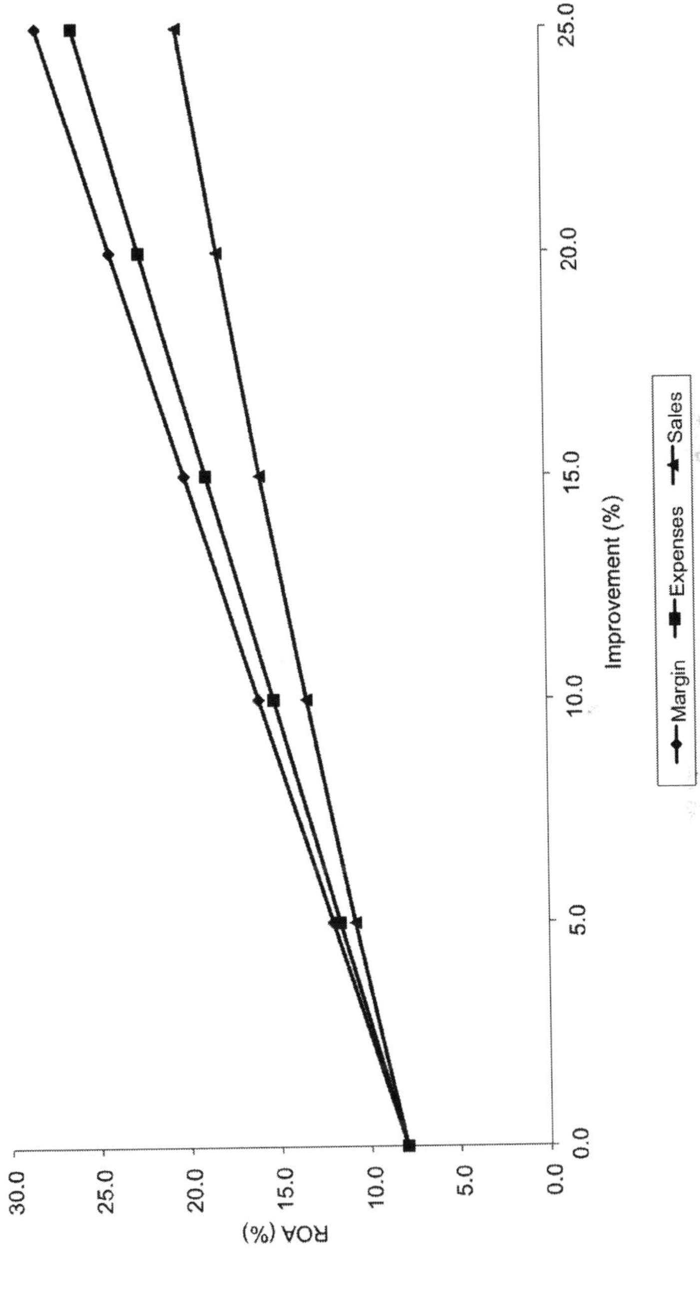

least try to find some specific avenues for margin enhancement rather than simply admitting defeat.

Making it Up with Volume

There are readers of this book, and you know who you are, who believe that the typical distributor can make it up with volume in its existing business structure. Those readers must once again be referred to by their title: Sales Manager.

Actually, the Sales Managers are right. Distributors can make it up with volume. In doing so, however, the firm will have to make a few minor adjustments. Getting rid of the sales force is one such adjustment that immediately springs to mind. Gutting the other expense categories is also required. An unpleasant thought for everybody in the firm except for the CFO who thinks it is a marvelous idea.

To understand the difficulties associated with making it up with volume, it is necessary to take another look at the economics of our old friend Mountain View Distributing. Given that there will be some serious changes in sales volume, it is necessary to focus on the fixed versus variable expense distinction for the moment.

Exhibit 17 looks at the impact on Mountain View of a 5.0% price cut. To see how it plays out, the price cut will be implemented for the entire firm. If the price cut were limited to only a select group of customers, it would have the same type of impact as shown in Exhibit 17. It would simply occur for part of the firm and not the total one. There will be no change in the conclusion to be drawn. Using the entire firm makes the analysis much easier to understand.

The first column of numbers in Exhibit 17, as usual, represents where Mountain View is right now. It includes some operating metrics at the top and an income statement at the bottom. All of the numbers have been seen before. The only item that deserves special mention is that variable expenses are assumed to be 5.0% of sales. These expenses—sales commissions and the like—will rise and fall in proportion to sales and will always be exactly 5.0% of sales volume.

The final two columns of numbers reflect the impact of a 5.0% price cut (total firm) under two very different scenarios. The first scenario assumes that as a reward for cutting its prices the firm experiences absolutely no increase in physical sales volume. This may seem like a lame assumption, but it is not.

The research associated with price wars indicates that market share changes derived from aggressive pricing action are infuriatingly modest. This is true as

Exhibit 17
The Impact of a 5.0% Price Cut
Under Two Assumptions About Sales Growth
Mountain View Distributing, Inc.

| | | --------5.0% Price Cut-------- | |
| | | No Sales | Sales |
Transaction Information	Current	Increase	Increase
Average Transaction	$500.00	$475.00	$475.00
Cost per Transaction	$375.00	$375.00	$375.00
Number of Transactions	40,000	40,000	52,459
Income Statement			
Net Sales	$20,000,000	$19,000,000	$24,918,033
Cost of Goods Sold	15,000,000	15,000,000	19,672,131
Gross Margin	5,000,000	4,000,000	5,245,902
Expenses			
Fixed	3,500,000	3,500,000	3,500,000
Variable (5.0% of Sales)	1,000,000	950,000	1,245,902
Total Expenses	4,500,000	4,450,000	4,745,902
Profit Before Taxes	$500,000	-$450,000	$500,000

long as competitors are in the *same general type of business*. That means they provide products and services in a similar manner. Price competition across industries (Amazon online versus Barnes & Noble retail stores) is a completely different issue. The obvious reason that price competition is a slow grind is that competitors yield ground on sales because of price competition very grudgingly. It becomes the proverbial Battle of Verdun.[16]

The second scenario assumes that *physical* volume increases by 31.1%. Well, there is a nice round number for you. Don't panic, it is merely a what-if exercise. The underlying assumption, though, is that competitors lie down peacefully and let Mountain View gain all the market share it wants. Basically, the competitors are all now managed by Neville Chamberlain.

A Price Cut with No Gain in Volume

In the first scenario, the average transaction falls from $500 to $475, a decline of 5.0%. The number of units sold stays constant. This means that dollar sales also decline by 5.0%. The firm is selling the same amount of merchandise at a price that is 5.0% lower.

---

[16] This reference is so obscure even the author had to look it up. However, it is the best analogy for a war of attrition which is what price competition becomes. The battle lasted for ten months resulting in an estimated 976,000 casualties. Neither side gained any territory. Sounds a lot like price competition in distribution.

The price the firm pays to its suppliers for merchandise does not fall. The firm is buying the same exact group of products from the same suppliers at the same prices as before. The result of this is that cost of goods sold remains the same as it was originally. The same cost per transaction times the same number of transactions results in the same cost of goods sold.

Gross margin is decimated. Note carefully that the dollar decline in gross margin ($1.0 million) is exactly the same as the dollar decline in sales. Every dollar of a price cut (absent an increase in physical volume for the moment) is a dollar of gross margin that also goes away.

There is some minor expense relief. Variable expenses are 5.0% of a smaller number so they fall right along with sales. Fixed expenses are, as always, fixed. The vaunted expense relief really is minor.

The punch line of the bad joke is that profit falls from a positive one ($500,000) to a negative one (-$450,000). Statistically, a decline of $950,000 or 190.0%. Always look on the bright side of life; the firm's tax bill has been slashed to zero.

In short, even a modest price reduction without an offsetting increase in physical volume does irreparable harm to the firm. This is not an academic concept. The reality is that most efforts to cut price in distribution create something very akin to this result.

A Price Cut with a Gain in Volume

The last column of numbers examines the fact that when prices are cut, physical volume jolly well better increase. Large increases in volume are a lot better than small ones.

As was stated earlier, physical volume in the last column is expected to increase by the awkward figure of 31.1%. With any luck there is a method to the madness here, so let's move along.

A 31.1% increase in physical volume means that the firm is no longer handling 40,000 transactions; it is handling 52,459 of them. This is a lot more work, but when you are making it up with volume, sacrifices must be made. More work is what Sundays were made for.

Sadly, despite the new lower price and the 31.1% increase in physical volume, there is not (repeat not) a 31.1% increase in dollar sales. The increase in work is offset by the reduction in the price and dollar sales only increase by 24.6%. It is more, but some of the glamour is already starting to wear off the model. The firm had to do 31.1% more work to generate 24.6% more sales.

Interestingly (the author hopes) cost of goods sold increases by the same 31.1% as did the increase in physical volume. The firm must purchase enough product to cover 31.1% more physical volume and is paying the same prices as before. Another way of saying this is that the whole thing is beginning to look like a much better deal for the suppliers than it is for Mountain View.

Gross margin dollars increase, but at a glacial pace. Gross margin was originally $5,000,000 and is now $5,245,902, an increase of $245,902 or 4.9%. Even the Sales Manager is beginning to show the first subtle signs of concern.

Expenses follow the same pattern as before. Namely, fixed expenses remain constant while variable expenses are the same old 5.0% of sales. Collectively, they rise by the *exact same dollar amount* as gross margin—an increase of $245,902.

If both gross margin and expenses go up by the same amount, profit has to remain exactly where it was originally, at $500,000. The author really hates to pick nits, but it looks like the firm had to work 31.1% harder just to keep profit where it was.

Some Unresolved Problems—After all that work, it is confession time. The model has two serious problems. One of them the price-cutting enthusiasts have been screaming for. The other one they are silently ignoring.

The first problem is that when purchases are increased by 31.1% the firm might be able to pressure (or berate) suppliers to purchase those products a lot cheaper. The shorthand notation among purchasing agents is called "moving to Column E" on the supplier's price schedule. This oversight represents a legitimate complaint. However, it is only one side of the pricing coin.

The other side is that the firm experienced a 31.1% increase in sales, yet fixed expenses were not increased at all. If the firm could actually do that, it should fire 31.1% of its employees tomorrow morning. It is morbidly obese in terms of expenses.

Whether or not these two factors more or less balance out is an interesting question. Dr. Know It All can provide the usual insightful answer: "Beats the living daylights out of me." It depends upon the specific situation. However, the author is willing to wager his already-tainted professional reputation that the two factors are probably pretty close in terms of balancing out. Cut price 5.0%, sell 31.1% more and make the same amount of profit.

Generalizing the Analysis

Exhibit 17, which you foolishly thought you were going to enjoy, is but one firm with one set of economics. Some firms have a higher gross margin than Mountain View, others have a lower one. This reality is so overwhelmingly important that it must be addressed. It is the *only place* in the book where Mountain View cannot reasonably serve as a proxy for distribution as a whole.

Exhibit 18 generalizes Exhibit 17 to the entire free world. That is, it attempts to determine how much dollar sales will have to increase to offset any size price cut in order to leave dollar profit at exactly the same dollar amount as before the price cut. The exhibit can be applied to any firm with any gross margin percentage. A financial tour de force incidentally.

The left side of the exhibit lists the gross margin levels *prior to making a price cut*. The numbers have been scaled from 5.0% to 30.0%. That is about as low as most distributors go and almost as high as they go. Across the top are the price cuts themselves, listed from 1.0% to 25.0%. To keep the exhibit from looking like an Amtrak timetable, only a few price cuts have been selected for presentation.

Exhibit 18
The Percentage Increase in Sales
Required to Exactly Offset a Price Reduction
by Level of Original Gross Margin Percentage

Original Gross Margin (%)	1.0	2.0	5.0	10.0	20.0	25.0
			Size of the Price Reduction (%)			
5.0	31.6 %	94.1 %				
10.0	12.8	29.8	145.2 %			
15.0	7.7	16.9	59.4	369.6 %		
20.0	5.3	11.4	35.7	125.0		
25.0	3.9	8.3	24.6	71.4	1,500.0 %	
30.0	3.0	6.3	18.1	48.0	269.2	3,500.0 %

The exhibit can best be understood by allowing the author to gloat. Back in Exhibit 17 when prices were cut by 5.0%, the firm had to increase *dollar sales* by 24.6% to maintain dollar profit right where it was to begin with.

In Exhibit 18, a firm with a 25.0% gross margin (such as Mountain View) would have to increase its sales by the same 24.6% in order to maintain profit. This entire example is looking suspiciously consistent.[17]

There are two conclusions to be drawn from Exhibit 18. First, the lower the original gross margin percentage, the more the firm has to pump sales to offset a price cut. Looking at the 1.0% price cut column, a firm with a 5.0% gross margin to start with would have to increase dollar sales by 31.6%, while

---

[17] Consistent, but replete with assumptions. In fact, this exhibit has so many assumptions built into it that an entire appendix is required to cover them. A short appendix, but still an Appendix. We are now up to Appendix D. That many appendices give the book an undeserved cachet.

a firm with a 30.0% gross margin would only need a 3.0% sales increase to hold profit steady.

Second, the sales increases are not linear moving from left to right. The English translation: Mountain View needs a 24.6% increase in dollar sales to offset a 5.0% price cut. However, if the price cut is doubled to 10.0% the sales increase required does not double. Instead, it almost triples. It moves from 24.6% to 71.4%. The more the firm cuts, the tougher life gets in terms of making it up with volume.

With the expense structure unchanged, it is very difficult for distributors to cut prices and drive enough additional volume to offset the cut. It requires zombies for competitors that will blissfully allow the firm to take share. The reality of making price cutting work is much more complicated. Time for the Walmart model of life.

The Walmart Model in Distribution

In making the Walmart model work, two factors are absolutely essential. First, the firm must be sure it can drive significantly higher sales volume with the low-price strategy. Second, it must be able to sharply reduce its expense load. Both of these factors are necessary for success. Alas, neither one of them is sufficient in and of itself.

The need for both sales and expense control is outlined in **Exhibit 19**. For this analysis it is necessary to revert back to payroll and all other expenses as the expense breakout. This is not cheating. The author is not moving back and forth between expense concepts on a whim. As was stated before, once something more complicated than just a short-term sales volume change is being considered, there is a need to look at natural expense breakouts.

In the first column of numbers we once again see Mountain View prior to any changes. In the last three columns the firm is going to implement an across-the-board price reduction of 5.0%. It is doing so under three different assumptions. The first is a marked increase in sales, the second is a reduction in expenses and the third is enjoying both at the same time.

The volume-only scenario involves a 20.0% increase in physical volume. This is an arbitrary number, but seems reasonable in a market where competitors are not going to give ground easily. A 20.0% sales increase by itself would, of course, take the firm's sales from $20.0 million to $24.0 million. However, the 5.0% price reduction must be considered so sales fall back to $22.8 million ($20.0 million times 120.0% times 95.0%). Since this is a sales-only model, all expenses have been held constant even though expenses should increase with more sales. Profit declines to $300,000.

The expense scenario simply reduces sales by 5.0% (a 5.0% price cut with no increase in physical volume) while cutting expenses by 10.0%. This is not entirely slash and burn with regard to expenses. It is closer to a brutal fine-tuning of the expense load. It is a disaster as the $500,000 profit transforms into a $50,000 loss. Once again America wants to know, so: expenses would have to be reduced by 20.0% to keep profit at the original $500,000 level given a 5.0% price cut.

When both actions are brought to the party, profit can be strengthened significantly. The last column combines the 20.0% increase in sales with the 10.0% reduction in expenses to increase profit by exactly 50.0%, ending up at $750,000.

Whether this could be done is completely unknown. It is possible that the increase in sales volume would cause expenses to actually increase to service more volume. Similarly, reducing expenses might cause the elimination of some valuable services and sales would fall. This is painful to admit, but your guess about what would happen is as good as the author's.

What is not a guess is that both yin and yang are needed for success. A price cut for most distributors will necessitate both a substantial increase in sales and a purging of expenses in order to be successful. Making those assumptions and moving forward requires courage...or desperation. In fact, shifts such as the last column of Exhibit 19 are often initiated by firms facing bleak economic prospects with their existing profit model. When the status quo is really bad, try something new.

For the majority of distributors, suddenly changing the economic model represents too much of a gamble to be seriously considered. They are in a rut, but a fairly comfortable one. What is needed is a higher gross margin in the existing business. For those distributors it is necessary to remember the immortal words of legendary football coach Darrell Royal, "You dance with who brung ya." Don't change the business, change the pricing model.

Obliterating the Cost-Plus Mentality

The very first step in developing a realistic pricing model is to eliminate the cost-plus approach, or at least wound it badly. This thought is essential, even if the firm does not think it actually uses cost-plus. If it is cost-plus, list less or any other pricing algorithm, prices are set in relationship to the product's cost.

Distributors still have to put a price on everything they sell. If there are thousands of SKUs needing a price, shortcuts must be implemented. More

Exhibit 19
The Impact of a 5% Price Cut
Under Different Sales and Expense Assumptions
Mountain View Distributing, Inc.

Income Statement ($)	Current Results	-5.0% Price Cut		
		Volume Increase	Expense Cut	Volume and Expense
Net Sales	$20,000,000	$22,800,000	$19,000,000	$22,800,000
Cost of Goods Sold	15,000,000	18,000,000	15,000,000	18,000,000
Gross Margin	5,000,000	4,800,000	4,000,000	4,800,000
Expenses				
Payroll and Fringe Benefits	3,000,000	3,000,000	2,700,000	2,700,000
All Other Expenses	1,500,000	1,500,000	1,350,000	1,350,000
Total Expenses	4,500,000	4,500,000	4,050,000	4,050,000
Profit Before Taxes	$500,000	$300,000	-$50,000	$750,000

Income Statement (%)				
Net Sales	100.0	100.0	100.0	100.0
Cost of Goods Sold	75.0	78.9	78.9	78.9
Gross Margin	25.0	21.1	21.1	21.1
Expenses				
Payroll and Fringe Benefits	15.0	13.2	14.2	11.8
All Other Expenses	7.5	6.6	7.1	5.9
Total Expenses	22.5	19.7	21.3	17.8
Profit Before Taxes	2.5	1.3	-0.3	3.3

often than not this involves adding some reasonable markup onto the costs for a group of somewhat similar items.

That is, items in a specific product category with similar sales levels all get the same markup. It allows the firm to move on with life. Some firms will make the issue somewhat more sophisticated by adjusting prices (usually down) for different customer groups. Essentially though, there is a standardized, fixed markup for similar items.

To understand the problem with this, it is necessary to recall your crazy Uncle Bob. He was the wild uncle you liked for some reason. He died last year and left you all of his worldly possessions in a cardboard box. A wild and crazy life doesn't lead to a lot of possessions.

Most of the stuff in the box was absolute junk. However, towards the bottom was a 1952 Topps Mickey Mantle rookie baseball card in pristine condition. No reasonably sane person would say, "let me figure out what it cost Uncle Bob (that would be 5¢, which not only included the card but a piece of bubble gum that had the look, feel and taste of linoleum) and then apply a reasonable markup to determine what I will sell it for."

Everybody would start by investigating the current market value of the card, which is around $250,000.[18] That means basing the price of the product on the *value* to the potential buyer. If that can be done in personal life, then it should be done in business. The difficulty is the same as was just discussed. Firms don't price one individual baseball card and then price nothing ever again. They price thousands of SKUs. The luxury of thinking about SKUs one at a time is just that, a luxury.

Getting to the issue of standard markups is going to require a circuitous route through the economics of buying and selling. Buy low, sell high is a great battle cry to rally the troops. To mix metaphors yet again, it needs a little more flesh on the bones.

Buying Low versus Selling High

Buying low and selling high are both essential activities for distributors. However, from an economic perspective, is the firm better off buying lower or selling higher? Doing both would be best of course, but don't get greedy.

Retreating back to an emotional perspective, this is no contest. Buying lower is a lot better because the firm doesn't have to raise its prices and risk the

---

[18] This particular card is the all-time favorite of counterfeiters. If Uncle Bob had 50 more such cards in the bottom of the cardboard box, then cost-plus is not such a bad idea after all.

potential wrath of customers. Besides, as every distributor well knows, "suppliers are making more money than they can figure out how to spend—giving distributors a deal won't hurt them."

From an economic perspective, though, the relationship is flipped. Selling higher is fundamentally better than buying lower. That point is reflected in **Exhibit 20**. For the exhibit some short-term volume changes are necessary, so the fixed versus variable expense concept once again rears its ugly head.

The first column of numbers is the obligatory "where the firm is now" column. The next column looks at buying lower while the final column examines selling higher. In both instances the change is exactly 2.0%. That is Mountain View will either buy *everything* 2.0% lower or sell *everything* 2.0% higher.

Exhibit 20
The Impact of Buying Lower or Selling Higher
Mountain View Distributing, Inc.

Income Statement	Current	Buying Lower	Selling Higher
Net Sales	$20,000,000	$20,000,000	$20,400,000
Cost of Goods Sold	15,000,000	14,700,000	15,000,000
Gross Margin	5,000,000	5,300,000	5,400,000
Expenses			
Fixed	3,500,000	3,500,000	3,500,000
Variable (5.0% of Sales)	1,000,000	1,000,000	1,020,000
Total Expenses	4,500,000	4,500,000	4,520,000
Profit Before Taxes	$500,000	$800,000	$880,000

Both columns are relatively straightforward. With buying lower, sales stays the same while there is a 2.0% cut in cost of goods sold. Since there is no increase in sales there is no increase in the variable expenses. The entire reduction in COGS, which was $300,000 ($15.0 million times 2.0%), goes right to the bottom line.

Selling higher is only slightly more complicated. Sales increase by 2.0% or $400,000. Since COGS will stay constant, the entire amount goes to the gross margin line. However, it must be stripped of some of its dignity before it hits the bottom line.

Variable expenses continue to be 5.0% of sales. With more sales, even though it is not more physical volume, there are increased variable expenses.

The increase is $20,000; the same exact 2.0% that sales increased.

Even with losing the $20,000, though, $380,000 goes to the bottom line. Profit is now $80,000 higher than buying low, or in percentage terms, 10.0% more. The brilliant conclusion from all this is that buying things cheaper is nifty. Selling them higher is niftier.

Taking it to the Street—At this point the casual reader may be concerned as to where exactly this is going. The answer is back to the concept of a fixed markup. We are heading there on a dead run. That dash ends at **Exhibit 21**.

That exhibit looks at the reality of closely relating prices to costs via some variation of cost-plus. The first two columns of numbers in the exhibit are identical to Exhibit 20. For those with a short attention span, a reminder is necessary. Buying merchandise 2.0% better drove profit up to $800,000. It was a very big deal at the time. It still is.

Exhibit 21
The Impact of Taking Buying Better Actions
to the Street
Mountain View Distributing, Inc.

	Current	Buying Lower	Tying Price to Cost
Net Sales	$20,000,000	$20,000,000	$19,600,000
Cost of Goods Sold	15,000,000	14,700,000	14,700,000
Gross Margin	5,000,000	5,300,000	4,900,000
Expenses			
Fixed	3,500,000	3,500,000	3,500,000
Variable (5.0% of Sales)	1,000,000	1,000,000	980,000
Total Expenses	4,500,000	4,500,000	4,480,000
Profit Before Taxes	$500,000	$800,000	$420,000

It is now time to investigate what happens in reality when that nice juicy improvement in buying takes place. Time to quote ol' coach Darrell Royal twice in one chapter: "Three things can happen...and two of 'em are bad."

The good thing is for the firm to put the profit generated from better buying in its pocket and not make any stupid decisions after the fact. Take the money and run so to speak. This is what should be done, but human nature once again gets in the way.

The second thing that could happen is that the distributor decides to leverage lower purchasing prices into lower selling prices to bring competitors to their knees. This blissfully ignores the fact that those competitors are probably buying better too.

The third thing is that the firm mechanistically enters the new, lower-cost price into its twenty-first century software system and lowers the selling price based upon a static markup model. This is yet another example of technology helping generate a stupid answer more quickly than could be done manually.

In either of the last two cases the final column of numbers in Exhibit 21 emerges. The firm has effectively taken the lower costs associated with effective buying "to the street." For some reason a lot of managers view this as a neutral profit action. "Hey we got to show customers we are price aggressive and it didn't cost us anything."

Au contraire (French for "next time use a calculator"). Sales is a bigger number than cost of goods sold. When both a big number and a smaller number are reduced by the same 2.0%, disaster strikes. Gross margin falls by (get ready to be impressed) 2.0% or $100,000. There is a decline in variable expenses, but it doesn't help much. Profit falls by $80,000.

This is pretty much reverse alchemy. Gold has been turned back into straw. Buying better and leaving well enough alone would have produced a $300,000 increase in profit. Taking it to the street reduces profit by $80,000. It is only a $380,000 swing for a firm making $500,000 to start with.

The Opportunity with Price Increases

When things are reversed and prices are rising consistently, cost-plus actually produces a positive impact. However, once again many firms can't leave well enough alone so it may not be all milk and honey. Given that over the long run prices tend to go up, this needs to be fully appreciated.

Exhibit 22 looks at the economics of a 5.0% supplier price increase. The usual distributor response to this is "the suppliers have done it to us again." Actually, sending a thank-you note to the supplier would be more appropriate.

The first column of numbers is the increasingly-redundant current results. The last three columns examine different responses to the price increase. They produce very different profit levels.

This second column is labeled Percent Pass Through but should be labeled Don't Ever Do Anything But This. It involves passing through a 5.0% outbound price increase because of the 5.0% inbound supplier price increase. In doing so, sales, cost of goods and gross margin all increase by 5.0%. Even with the automatic increase in variable expenses, profit rises to $700,000.

What this means is that when suppliers increase prices their distributors should kiss their ring. The distributor makes a lot more money. On top of that, the distributor can also blame the price increase on the idiot supplier. The best of all possible worlds.

Exhibit 22
Why Supplier Price Increases are Beneficial
Mountain View Distributing, Inc.

| | Current | -------------5.0% Price Increase------------- | | |
		Percent Pass Through	Dollar Pass Through	Increase Partially Absorbed
Net Sales	$20,000,000	$21,000,000	$20,750,000	$20,600,000
Cost of Goods Sold	15,000,000	15,750,000	15,750,000	15,750,000
Gross Margin	5,000,000	5,250,000	5,000,000	4,850,000
Expenses				
Fixed	3,500,000	3,500,000	3,500,000	3,500,000
Variable (5.0% of Sales	1,000,000	1,050,000	1,037,500	1,030,000
Total Expenses	4,500,000	4,550,000	4,537,500	4,530,000
Profit Before Taxes	$500,000	$700,000	$462,500	$320,000
Profit Before Taxes	2.5%	3.3%	2.2%	1.6%
Change in Profit (%)		40.0%	-7.5%	-36.0%

In the real world (which the author tries to avoid) panic about raising prices sets in. If it were only one SKU going up in price then the software system belittled earlier could simply apply the same set markup and raise the price of the item by 5.0%. Unfortunately, it is usually an entire product line or an entire product segment going up. It is big and it is noticeable. We know that our customers will abandon us in droves if we raise prices across the board.

The most common response is the third column of numbers labeled Dollar Pass Through. Prices outbound are increased by the same *dollar* amount as the inbound prices have been increased by the supplier. Percent for percent has been replaced by dollar for dollar.

Since cost of goods increased by $750,000 with the 5.0% supplier price increase, sales will increase by the same dollar amount. As a result, the gross margin dollars remain exactly where they were. With regard to profit, it is close to a push, but because of those pesky variable expenses profit actually falls slightly, to $462,500. A major profit opportunity is lost.

When competition is hot and heavy, firms often retreat to a partial pass through. Strategically this is trying to find the amount of a price increase that will not cause any customer complaints. In the final column of numbers, labeled Increase Partially Absorbed, prices have been increased by 3.0% (an arbitrary example) while inbound product costs increased by 5.0%. By this point every reader should anticipate disaster and it arrives right on schedule. Profit falls to $320,000.

All of this leads to a two-pronged strategy. When the firm buys better (or prices simply fall), take the money and run. When prices are rising, follow the percent for percent price increase formula. So easy to understand, so difficult to do. Somewhat akin to staying sober when the in-laws visit.

Pricing for Profit

Finally, time to address a pricing algorithm that (1) moves away from mindless cost-plus, (2) allows the firm to be competitive, and (3) drives a slightly higher gross margin percentage. This algorithm will be called "stretching the price matrix." It doesn't really require brains (since the author is presenting it), but it does require guts and a fairly sizeable chunk of time.

To get started it is necessary to review the multitude of items in the assortment. It doesn't make any difference if the firm carries 1,000 SKUs or 75,000 SKUs; the mix of items looks suspiciously like **Exhibit 23**. The numbers are for Mountain View, but the underlying concept applies to everybody.

	Exhibit 23 A Velocity Code Analysis of the Items Carried Mountain View Distributing, Inc.			
Velocity Code	**Percent of Sales**	**Percent of SKUs**	**Gross Margin %**	
A+	10.0	2.0	10.0	
A	50.0	8.0	20.0	
B	20.0	20.0	25.0	
C	15.0	20.0	40.0	
D	5.0	50.0	60.0	
Total	100.0	100.0	25.0	

Traditional Matrix Pricing

Most distributors have an A through D (sometimes even A through H) product grouping designation. These letters, called Velocity Codes, provide an idea of how fast the items sell. A items are tonnage items and D items are, woefully, slow sellers or the infamous dogs.

Exhibit 23 expands the traditional velocity code designation by adding an even faster-selling group of items designated here as A+. In essence these are the fastest of the fastest selling.

The exhibit ranks items using the simplest of methods. All of the SKUs are sorted from the single SKU with the most dollar sales during a period (typically a year) down to the final SKU with the least amount of dollar sales during the same time period. It doesn't make any difference again if it is 1,000 SKUs or 75,000 SKUs; there is now a parade of SKUs ranked from highest dollar sales to lowest.

The SKUs that provide the top 10.0% of sales are assigned an A+ ranking here, the next 50.0% of sales are A items and so on down the list, until the D items which provide the very last 5.0% of sales. All of the A+ items will generate nice big sales during the year, such as, say $20,000. All of the D items will generate a little bitty sales number like $2.00 or even worse, $0.00.

Exhibit 23 demonstrates that the Percent of SKUs relationship is the mirror image of the Percent of Sales Relationship. That is, the A+ items which generate 10.0% of total dollar sales only represent 2.0% of the firm's total SKU count. A few items; lots of sales.

At the other extreme, 50.0% of all SKUs are D items, but they only generate 5.0% of sales volume. The other categories are somewhere in between. The A items have more sales than SKUs, relatively speaking, the C and D items have more SKUs than sales and the B items are exactly equal in terms of sales and SKUs.

Pricing Implications—The pricing implication comes from the final column of numbers which looks at the gross margin percentage on each of the categories. In a prototype Matrix Pricing or Velocity Pricing (interchangeable terms) world, the fast-selling items have a low gross margin percentage and the dogs have a very high one. To appreciate the implication for pricing, some thought needs to be given to the nature of these items.

A+ items—These are the items (SKUs) that are absolutely pure commodities. That is, customers purchase them on a frequent basis, it is effortless for customers to compare prices between distributors and therefore pricing becomes extremely important. To a real extent, any firm that is higher than its competition on the A+ items might as well rent a billboard on the interstate and announce in big block letters: "We Are High on Everything We Sell."[19] The A+ items are where firms establish their price bona fides.

A sad way to think about the A+ items is that the firm has almost no control over their pricing. If competitors lower prices, the firm really has to follow suit. That means the firm's prices are set by either its dumbest competitor

---

[19] The author lives in Colorado. With recent changes in recreational drug regulations in the state, this statement can be interpreted in numerous ways.

or its smartest one. In either case, the firm is a victim of the market. For Mountain View the A+ items have a gross margin percentage of 10.0%.

A Items—The author has frequently referred to the A items as semi-commodities. Since this is somewhat analogous to semi-pregnant, it is a less than brilliant designation. It will have to do. A items are still price sensitive, but not to the extent of the A+ items. They are not bought quite as frequently as A+ items and price information is more diffuse. The gross margin percentage for these in Exhibit 23 is 20.0%. This is matrix pricing in action—the faster the sales rate the lower the gross margin percentage.

B Items—Let's try a mnemonic: B stands for Basics. These items account for 20.0% of the SKUs and generate 20.0% of the sales. Their gross margin percentage is 25.0% which is exactly equal to that of the total firm. To know the B items is to know the entire company.

C items—At this point we are moving towards the bottom of the barrel. These items are decidedly slower sellers. However, they are not arthritic, just somewhat slow—about 20.0% of the SKUs and only 15.0% of the sales. Meanwhile the gross margin percentage is getting into the interesting range of 40.0%. Oh, if we could just sell more of them.

D Items—Finally, for your viewing pleasure, we have the D items. They are fully half of the SKUs but a miniscule 5.0% of the firm's dollar sales. There is a real temptation to get rid of these items. Resist that temptation for now. As an aid in resisting the temptation, take a look at the gross margin percentage of 60.0%. Three thoughts follow from the 60.0% margin, not all of them random.

First and foremost, these items must generate some very nice profit when they are sold. The fact that they don't sell very often is disquieting, of course, but a 60.0% gross margin borders on a license to steal.

A second observation is one that is pervasive among salespeople. Namely, we are over-charging our poor defenseless customers on these items. That logic, spurious as it is, drives from the fact that A+ items are sold with a gross margin of 10.0%. Surely 60.0% is too high. Well, actually, it is too low, but that discussion must wait for a few more paragraphs.

Third, there is the thought that even with a high gross margin percentage the items might not be worth it. If a D items sells for $2.00, then the firm only generates $1.20 in margin which has to cover the expenses of picking the item off the shelf, assembling, delivery etc.

Maybe the firm would be better off getting rid of the puny little D items and investing more in A items. Sell an A item for $50 with a 20.0% gross margin and there is $10.00 of margin to cover said picking, assembling and the like.

This final thought must be held in anticipation (eager or meager, depending upon the reader) until Chapter Six. For right now all attention must be given to pricing.

Stretching the Price Matrix

If the firm is going to generate a reasonable margin in a price-sensitive world, it must engage in what was referred to earlier as stretching the price matrix. What this means is that the ratio of the highest gross margin percentage category (D) to the lowest (A+) needs to be widened. At present the ratio for Mountain View is 6 to 1 (60.0% in relationship to 10.0%).

There are two ways to stretch the matrix. The first is to lower the gross margin percentage on the A+ items. Not the most brilliant idea ever. Ranks right up there with "let's go over to the Watergate and see what the Democrats are up to." Remember that the prices on the A+ items are set by either the smartest or dumbest competitor. Either way, leave well enough alone.

The key is to raise the prices on the D items. For that action every firm needs a marketing slogan with regard to the D items. That slogan is: *Hose 'Em.* That would appear to be a disgusting phrase. It actually isn't, but for right now assume it is disgusting. Unless you are Mother Teresa incarnate, get over it. Repeat it with the author: *Hose 'Em.*

To help get over the fear of hosing, it is useful to go back to Exhibit 23 and look at the A+ and A items. On those two groups—which constitute 60.0% of the firm's sales—the distributor is the hosee. That 60.0% of sales is all going out the door at a below-average gross margin percentage. Very possibly it is going out the door at a margin that is lower than the cost of selling and handling the products.

Distributors must come to the stark reality that at some point it absolutely must be their turn to hold the hose. All that is required is to hold the hose a lousy 5.0% of the time. If that can't be done, there is never going to be enough profit.

On top of that the firm may not be hosing at all. Conceptually, the firm held the item in inventory for a year waiting for this customer to need it. When the customer did need it, the distributor had it in stock. That isn't hosing, that is providing tremendous added value. Since hosing sounds so incredibly clever to the author, let's stick with it.

There are two aspects to hosing. The first is how much you can hose. The second is when you can hose them without them knowing they are being hosed. The answer, then the analysis: You can hose a lot when you do hose, but you can't hose very often.

Raising Prices—The magnitude of the hosing opportunity is shown in **Exhibit 24**. The left half of the exhibit lists all of the velocity code categories along with the current sales dollars, gross margin dollars and gross margin percentage. The blended gross margin remains at 25.0%, which is generated via gross margins ranging from 10.0% to 60.0% in the price matrix.

| | -------Current Results------- | | | ----Selective Price Increases---- | | |
| | | ---Gross Margin--- | | | ---Gross Margin--- | |
Velocity Code	Sales	Dollars	Percent	Sales	Dollars	Percent
A+	$2,000,000	$200,000	10.0	$2,000,000	$200,000	10.0
A	10,000,000	2,000,000	20.0	10,000,000	2,000,000	20.0
B	4,000,000	1,000,000	25.0	4,000,000	1,000,000	25.0
C	3,000,000	1,200,000	40.0	3,000,000	1,200,000	40.0
D	1,000,000	600,000	60.0	1,100,000	700,000	63.6
Total	$20,000,000	$5,000,000	25.0	$20,100,000	$5,100,000	25.4

Exhibit 24
Stretching the Price Matrix
Mountain View Distributing, Inc.

On the right hand side of the exhibit, prices have been left alone on the A+, A, B and C categories. However, on the D items, which represent a miniscule 5.0% of sales volume, prices have been increased by 10.0%. Looking across the D item row, sales increased from $1.0 million to $1.1 million on the D items.

It is now big assumption time. In the exhibit, increasing prices did not cause unit sales to fall. That assumption will be defended brilliantly and fearlessly shortly. Stay with the numbers for right now.

Since the sales increase is generated as a result of the price increase, all of the sales increase ($100,000) is also a gross margin increase. The gross margin is now an unconscionable (but profitable) 63.6% on the D items and 25.4% for the total firm. And it's just that easy.

It is essential to remember that since the firm is not actually moving more product tonnage, the entire $100,000 of additional gross margin dollars pretty much goes to the bottom line. There are always those irascible variable expenses of course. They are still 5.0% of sales. Taking them into consideration, only $95,000 goes to the bottom line. That increases Mountain View's pretax bottom line by 19.0% without doing any more work. What's not to like?

The problem at gut-check time is that nobody really believes that prices can be raised by 10.0% on the D items without the firm being forced out of business by price-sensitive customers who abandon the firm en masse to seek better prices from competitors.

In every distribution organization there are a lot of opportunities to engage in value pricing. Those opportunities are surprisingly easy to find. In point of fact, they are listed in **Exhibit 25**, or at least their characteristics are.

Distributors need to look for what are commonly called blind items. They are all over the blooming place so they shouldn't be hard to find. Blind items in their purest form have two ideal characteristics: (1) nobody knows what the price should be, and (2) nobody cares.

The difficulty is that blind items are not designated on the side of the carton: *Blind Item Inside, Raise Price Accordingly.* Management must hunt relentlessly for blind items. Much less fun than Easter eggs, but a lot more profitable.

Exhibit 25
The Common Characteristics of Blind Items

Characteristic	Implication
Low Sales Level	Bought rarely, unlikely to remember the last price paid
Not Heavily Promoted	Information about price not readily available
Bought Only When Needed	Availability more important than price
Low Price	On a small item, no real concern about price
Repair Parts	Buy something small, avoid buying something large
Unusual	Hard to find, availability is key
Non-Seasonal	No need to discount "in season"
Unbranded	Difficult to obtain specific price information

The exhibit lists eight hints that an item might be a blind one along with a lame explanation of the reasoning behind each factor. The more of these factors an individual item has, the more likely it is to actually be a blind item. As a general rule, items with four or more of these characteristics are almost certainly blind items. Those with three or more are probably blind items.

Of all the characteristics of blind items listed in Exhibit 25, the two that pop up almost every time are Low Sales Level and Bought Only When Needed. These are the stock-in-trade of D items. These also are items for which the incredible value added that the distributor provides is that the item is actually available. It is not a good value added, it is a sensational one. The firm deserves a higher margin on them.

The challenge is to have the guts to raise the prices. Hey, if it is an item for which nobody knows the price and nobody cares, what's the downside risk? That downside risk is that when one customer out of a thousand complains about the price on a blind item, the entire firm goes into panic mode. If there are *never* any price complaints, the firm is engaged in self-immolation via under-pricing.

Running and Hiding Once Again—In Chapter One it was suggested that firms not only had to deal with operational factors to be best of breed. They also had to have a market position that allowed them to run and hide from competition.

The entire concept of generating a higher gross margin through blind-item pricing is the personification of running and hiding. The firm is price competitive on tonnage items. However, when it drives higher margins on slower selling items that are bought on the basis of need, competition does not see anything.

It is also useful to remember from Chapter One (assuming anybody can) that one of the two strategic drivers of profitability was avoiding commoditization. Raising prices on blind items very subtly shifts the overall dollar sales mix (but not the unit movement) out of commodities.

Moving Forward to Chapter Five

Gross margin will probably be the most frustrating of all the CPVs. It has a huge impact on profit. At the same time, it is always the most difficult factor to bring under control. Price competition always seems to get in the way.

If firms can remember to pocket the savings from special buying opportunities and raise prices percent for percent when supplier prices go up, they are well on the way to generating that small improvement in margin that pays such big dividends. Finally, it should be remembered that on blind items, product availability is much more important than price—even for the most price-driven customer.

With sales, expense and margin controls firmly in place, the firm should be in line for the better profit results that are its due. At this point it is time for the problem children in the sales force to do their job and destroy everything that was so carefully constructed.

CliffsNotes™ Discussion of Chapter Four

- Gross margin is the most important driver of profit.
- Unless firms want to change the entire nature of their business, making it up with volume is an extremely difficult proposition.

- In driving a higher margin, buying low and selling high are both good, but selling high is an even better idea than buying low.
- In order to drive a higher margin in a competitive market, firms need to find ways to stretch the price matrix.
- To stretch the price matrix the firm must find blind items and actually re-price them—a somewhat labor-intensive activity.

5 Sales Force Abdication

Given the title of the chapter it is logical to assume that it will make fun of the sales force. That is not correct; it will belittle the sales force. Actually, it will only belittle that small, but brutally destructive, part of the sales force that negates all of the profit that the majority of the sales force works so hard to create.

Let's start with a given. Salespeople have one of the most difficult jobs in the entire firm. Salespeople must understand customer needs, be comfortable discussing an extensive product line, monitor seasonal trends, assist in maintaining control over pricing and transmit information between the company and customers on a myriad of issues. Oh yes, one other thing, the suckers are supposed to meet quota.

This vast array of requisite skill sets leads to one important point that permeates the entire chapter. Namely, too many salespeople aren't.

Do not ask aren't what. The last sentence was complete in and of itself. Too many people who are in sales actually aren't qualified to be salespeople. This is not a character failing. This is simply a fact of life regarding supply and demand.

The American economy requires a lot of salespeople to keep functioning. In point of fact, it requires a lot more than there is in the way of quality raw material to fill that need. It is a classic supply-side constraint issue. A significant proportion of people in sales positions do not have the complete skill set required to be effective salespeople. They may well be qualified to be outstanding in other positions. Just not sales.

Research conducted by The Profit Planning Group suggests that for any selected group of ten salespeople they will break as follows:

- **Superstars**—Actually, this should be singular. This is the one out of ten individuals who produces sales revenue far in excess of the typical salesperson. This individual in many cases is also a blasted prima donna. The person you hate but can't do without.

- **Strong Performers**—Two additional salespeople who generate above-average sales, but don't come within striking distance of the top performer. They typically generate their above-average level of sales without incident or theatrics.
- **Soldiers**—These represent half of the total sales force. They are typical in almost every aspect. They represent the exact average in terms of a wide range of sales metrics, such as sales per salesperson, gross margin percentage, new accounts opened, sick days taken and everything else.
- **Sales Laggards**—The last two salespeople in the mix are the real problems in the sales team. Their sales productivity is well below the norm for the total firm. They are hurting the firm in ways that are not fully appreciated, even in firms with strong sales force control systems.

This objective of this chapter is to shed light on the way that poor sales performance impacts profitability. To do so, the chapter is organized into three sections:

- **Accepting Inadequate Performance**—Understanding why distributors, unlike many other organizations, have a natural tendency to carry poor performers longer than they should.
- **The Economics of Poor Sales Performance**—An examination of exactly how inadequate sales generation—in relationship to potential sales—hurts profit performance as well as a discussion as to why the impact on performance is chronically underestimated.
- **Improving Sales Force Performance**—A brief discussion of some of the mechanisms that must be put in place in order to ensure proper sales results.[20]

Accepting Inadequate Performance

No distributor would tolerate terrible sales performance from a salesperson. The reality, though, is that there is an inherent tolerance for mediocre performance. The tolerance derives directly from the fact that distribution organizations are managed by human beings. Once again, the source of all problems in the world takes center stage.

---

[20] For some strategic insights into these issues, especially why compensation systems don't lead to sales growth, see Michael Marks and Mike Emerson, *What's Your Plan? Smart Salesforce Compensation in Wholesale Distribution,* National Association of Wholesaler-Distributors, 2012.

The problem of human failings has three distinct dimensions. The first is organizational. The structure of most distribution entities makes it difficult to eliminate problems. The second dimension is territorial. Until recently it was next to impossible to measure territory potential precisely to determine exactly who wasn't performing as desired. The third dimension is financial. There is a strong, and completely inaccurate, belief that commission-heavy compensation systems overcome minor sales force problems.

Organizational—The organizational problem has to do with the fact that in distribution the entities where salespeople are housed tend to be uniquely small. In a truly small distributor there may only be four or five salespeople. The CEO knows each and every one of them and knows the members of their family as well. Trouble brewing already.

As distributors grow, it would seem that they would become more impersonal. However, for most distributors an increase in sales size leads directly to branching. According to the *Cross-Industry Compensation Report*[21], the typical distributor's branch has five employees. Two of them are in outside sales.

In a large firm with numerous branches, the CEO may have no real idea who these two people are out there in Ottumwa. However, their direct contact is with the branch manager. Now it is the branch manager who knows each and every one of them as well as their family members.

Eliminating the poor performer, be they in sales or anywhere else, is incredibly difficult to do in small groups. It involves eliminating a nice person (the prima donna who is not nice is exempt anyway because of the massive sales generated). Not only is this person likeable, but will surely reach reasonable potential with just a little more training and support. Of course they will. Any day now.

In organizations with large-scale work units the termination decision is much easier. It requires nothing more than a list of employees and a magic marker. Eliminating 2,000 employees is actually a lot easier than terminating one employee that the manager interacts with every day. Branching provides for an unsurpassed customer-centric sales structure, but creates some interesting organizational problems.

Territorial—Poor salespeople can hide for an extended period of time behind the difficulty of estimating territory potential. Until recently the algorithms for assessing potential were crude. To often "Fred" (who really is a nice

---

[21] The Profit Planning Group, *Cross-Industry Compensation Report,* 2004, 2006, 2008, 2010, 2012, 2014, ad infinitum.

guy) was cut some slack due to the excuse that he is doing as well as he can in his inadequate territory.

Financial—The final factor leading to an acceptance of inadequate performance is the misguided belief that poor sales performance is bothersome rather than life threatening. The core of this belief is the fact that a very large proportion of total compensation for the typical salesperson comes from commissions. That means, when they don't generate adequate sales, they are viewed as hurting themselves a lot and the company a little bit. Better to accept the minor profit issue than go to the time, trouble and expense of finding a replacement.

Segmenting the Firm into Sales Territories

The organizational challenge, the difficulty in evaluating territories, and the belief in commissions as a shield from profit problems will be discussed at agonizing length in the next section. First it is necessary to look at the sales force from a profit and loss perspective to see if there really is anything to worry about. That happens in **Exhibit 26**.

Get ready to be astounded. The first column of numbers for Mountain View in the exhibit is actually different than it has been in the endless string of previous exhibits. The author pledges not to make this mistake again.

Exhibit 26
Financial Results per Salesperson
Mountain View Distributing, Inc.

Income Statement	Total Firm	Per Salesperson
Net Sales	$20,000,000	$2,000,000
Cost of Goods Sold	15,000,000	1,500,000
Gross Margin	5,000,000	500,000
Expenses		
Commissions (10.0% of GM)	500,000	50,000
Other Variable (2.5% of Sales)	500,000	50,000
Fixed	3,500,000	350,000
Total Expenses	4,500,000	450,000
Profit Before Taxes	$500,000	$50,000

Actually only two numbers are different. Sounds like no harm, no foul. The two different numbers arise because the exhibit splits variable expenses into two sub-parts. Since the beginning of Chapter One (68 days ago for the typical reader) variable expenses have been a monolithic 5.0% of sales. For understanding sales force economics, variable expenses have two very different components.

Most, but certainly not all, distributors pay commissions based upon gross margin rather than sales. To reflect this, the exhibit assumes that commissions are 10.0% of the firm's gross margin dollars. The variable expenses that are not commissions (bad debts, interest on accounts receivable, etc.) are 2.5% of sales volume.

The first column is now ready for public display. To get back to a predictable pattern, this is nothing more than a recapitulation of the total firm. Still $20.0 million in sales, still $500,000 in profit. Large numbers at the top, small ones at the bottom.

The second column breaks the total firm numbers down on a per salesperson basis. It is assumed that the firm has 10 salespeople. Consequently, this column merely divides the total firm numbers by 10 to generate a per salesperson figure. This does not mean that all salespeople are equal. This provides an average to use as a starting point.

This means the average salesperson generates $2.0 million in revenue and $500,000 in gross margin. With a 10.0% commission rate, the average salesperson receives $50,000 in commissions. This is on top of any base salary received that would be included in fixed expenses.

The picture is rounded out with the non-commission variable expenses which are 2.5% of sales and the fixed expenses which are assigned to all salespeople equally. At long last, the average profit per salesperson is $50,000.

Management knows all 10 of the salespeople personally and likes every one of them. Furthermore, there is no real profit downside as the sales force is paid on the basis of gross margin. All is right in the world. That world will remain calm and placid until about the middle of the next section.

The Economics of Poor Sales Performance

Ineffective salespeople impact company performance in two distinct ways. First, they do not generate the sales volume that they should from their territories. Second, they tend to cut prices as the only way to meet customer price objections. Both situations are disastrous, even if the performance slippages are rather modest.

Low Sales Generation

Exhibit 27 looks at the four categories of salespeople identified previously—superstars, strong performers, soldiers and sales laggards. There is one additional, and very important, item to remember while reviewing the exhibit: it is assumed that all territories are exactly equal in terms of sales *potential*.

That means that every territory, if properly serviced, would generate about $2.0 million in revenue for Mountain View. There may be $5.0 million in total revenue in the territory. With proper effort, Mountain View should get $2.0 million of that total.

This is yet another of the author's incredibly unrealistic assumptions. However, the assumption makes it much easier to see what is going on. It also means that the assignment of fixed expenses equally to each salesperson was not arbitrary or capricious. In this example every territory has equal potential.

In the first column of numbers, the one superstar generates 50.0% more in revenue than would a typical salesperson in the same territory. That means $3.0 million in revenue, not $2.0 million. This individual is taking serious hunks of volume from the competition.

The two strong performers are generating 20.0% more than expected, so they are also helping the firm gain a little market share. The soldiers are producing right at potential, so the firm's share is at parity. Finally, the two sales laggards are at 55.0% of potential. Another firm has "our" share.

These variations in performance are not contrived. The range of performance described above is 2.7 times (150 divided by 55). This is entirely consistent with proprietary research conducted by The Profit Planning Group for a large trade association. That research covered salespeople in several hundred firms. Such large variations in revenue generation held true even after allowing for differences in territory potential. Large ranges in sales performance are a fact of life. To repeat a pithy observation: Some salespeople aren't.

There is yet another issue that must be discussed before the narrative can weave its serpentine route to some sort of conclusion. It is assumed that all of the salespeople generate the same gross margin percentage of 25.0% of sales. In point of fact bad salespeople typically operate on a lower gross margin percentage than the good ones. That will be discussed later. One small step for mankind at a time.

Finally, the reason for this section. The superstar with the high level of sales volume is also producing a lot of gross margin dollars, $750,000 to be precise. That person is also receiving a handsome commission check, probably on top of a base salary.

Exhibit 27

Financial Performance by Type of Salesperson

Mountain View Distributing, Inc.

	Super-stars	Strong Performers	Soldiers	Sales Laggards	Total Firm
Salespeople (#)	1	2	5	2	10
Income Statement					
Net Sales	$3,000,000	$4,800,000	$10,000,000	$2,200,000	$20,000,000
Cost of Goods Sold	2,250,000	3,600,000	7,500,000	1,650,000	15,000,000
Gross Margin	750,000	1,200,000	2,500,000	550,000	5,000,000
Expenses					
Commissions (10.0% of GM)	75,000	120,000	250,000	55,000	500,000
Other Variable (2.5% of Sales)	75,000	120,000	250,000	55,000	500,000
Fixed	350,000	700,000	1,750,000	700,000	3,500,000
Total Expenses	500,000	940,000	2,250,000	810,000	4,500,000
Profit Before Taxes	$250,000	$260,000	$250,000	-$260,000	$500,000
Sales per Salesperson	$3,000,000	$2,400,000	$2,000,000	$1,100,000	$2,000,000
Profit per Salesperson	$250,000	$130,000	$50,000	-$130,000	$50,000
Total Profit	$250,000	$260,000	$250,000	-$260,000	$500,000
Percent of Total Firm Profit	50.0%	52.0%	50.0%	-52.0%	100.0%

Since all territories are the same, this individual is also covering 10.0% of the overhead expenses. Assuming that the net profit for this person can be calculated (a debate topic coming soon), the salesperson is driving $250,000 to the bottom line. That means that one salesperson is producing 50.0% of the profits of the total firm.

The two strong performers produce $260,000 in profit. The author's crude math indicates that these three folks (one superstar and two strong performers) are 30.0% of the sales team and are generating 102.0% of the firm's profit. It is enough to make Vilfredo Pareto and his 80/20 rule weep with joy.[22]

The solders are exactly typical. Those five good old boys (in sales even females are good old boys) represent half of the sales force and generate half of the profit. They are the exact average calculated before.

For those of you keeping score at home, we have an interesting situation. The three groups covered so far are providing 152.0% of the firm's profit. Something has to give somewhere.

Giving the Profit Back—The real issue is at the tail end of the parade. The two sales laggards represent a complete mess. In aggregate they account for a *loss* equal to 52.0% of total profits. Alas, they are really nice folks. In fact, one of them, Fred, is captain of the bowling team.

If it were 1995 once again and the real challenge facing distributors involved filling all those orders that kept coming in at the speed of light, the last two members of the sales force could be categorized as worrisome. If the new normal really is the new normal and distributors must fight for every dollar of revenue, it is several steps beyond worrisome.

The most salient point of this discussion is that for most firms, the $220,000 loss is never seen. To use the brilliant term coined by the author, the loss is the *Cost of Goods Not Sold*. That is, it represents the loss arising from poor sales performance. On a typical income statement, though, all that is ever seen is the $500,000 total profit. The $260,000 of *potential* additional profit remains hidden.

It is actually a lot worse than missing out on $260,000, though. If the two poor performers could be replaced by soldiers (stop dreaming about another superstar), then the $260,000 loss ($130,000 each) would be replaced by a

---

[22] Vilfredo Pareto had the original idea, but focused only on the income-distribution aspects. Joseph Juran, who had the advantage of being able to read Italian, took the concept and popularized "the vital few and the trivial many" (along with six sigma quality control and a lot of other powerful stuff). Joseph M. Juran, *Quality Control Handbook*, McGraw-Hill, 1951.

$100,000 profit ($50,000 each for soldiers). The potential net swing in profit is a modest $360,000 for a firm generating $500,000 in profit to begin with.

All Exhibit 27 says is that poor-performing salespeople kill the company. Wouldn't want to get rid of them, though. After all, salespeople are hard to find.

The idea of finding replacement salespeople, training them, and allowing them to slowly develop a territory causes firms to take the line of least resistance. Just keep the folks in place who are already there. Hey, they are on commission, so there is no real loss for the firm.

Price Cutting

Hide the kids. Price cutting is back as a topic. The avalanche of words devoted to price cutting in Chapter Four was not enough to sate the author's desire to bore every distribution executive in North America. Actually, there is a different perspective to price cutting here. It revolves around the theme of the previous section—salespeople are paid on commission, so what difference does it make?

Determining why salespeople are paid on commission is an interesting inquiry. The answer to that inquiry depends upon whether the analysis is conducted in the boardroom or the bar. In different terms, it depends upon whether management is dealing with platitudes or the raw truth.

In the boardroom, the platitude is that if salespeople are paid on gross margin it encourages them to sell up, increase their gross margin percentage and therefore their commission check. It is the sort of thing that can be put into the firm's goal statement. Sounds nice. There is an element of truth to that view, but also more than a little bit of bloviating.

The real impetus to pay salespeople on commission reflects a very cynical, but very valid, view of the lower end of the sales force. That view is that salespeople are often (always) under tremendous pressure to lower prices. Since they are under such pressure, some (sales laggards by name) will inevitably succumb. If they are paid on commission, they are killing their commission check and not really hurting the company. Kind of like the message regarding sales. Oh, that it were true.

To see the impact of price cutting at the sales force level, it is useful to visit **Exhibit 28**. The exhibit looks at the performance of one of the soldiers in the sales force. These were the folks who were exactly typical in their performance. These are not the individuals likely to cut price. However, it is always most illustrative to start from typical performance.

Exhibit 28
The Impact of Sales Force Price Cutting
With Commissions Based on Gross Margin
Mountain View Distributing, Inc.

| Income Statement | Current Results | -------5.0% Price Cut------ | |
		Traditional Commission	Sliding Commission
Net Sales	$2,000,000	$1,900,000	$1,900,000
Cost of Goods Sold	1,500,000	1,500,000	1,500,000
Gross Margin	500,000	400,000	400,000
Expenses			
Commissions (10.0% of GM)	50,000	40,000	-47,500
Other Variable (2.5% of Sales)	50,000	47,500	47,500
Fixed	350,000	350,000	350,000
Total Expenses	450,000	437,500	350,000
Profit Before Taxes	$50,000	-$37,500	$50,000

The first column simply reproduces those numbers from back in Exhibit 26. The last two columns look at the impact of a 5.0% price cut. The cut is across the board to highlight its impact. This issue of a 5.0% price cut has been addressed before (who amongst us can forget the inimitable Exhibit 17?). The key difference here is that the impact of the price cut is *buffered by a compensation plan* that involves a heavy commission component. That component is based upon gross margin rather than sales.

Traditional Commission Plan—In the middle column of numbers the firm pays a commission that is still 10.0% of gross margin, the same exact commission structure as before. It is a well-intentioned, but ineffective, way to punish price cutting.

With a 5.0% price cut, the sales generated falls by $100,000. It should be remembered from the previous chapter that every dollar of sales loss from a price cut is also a dollar of gross margin loss. That means that the margin dollars generated fall to $400,000; a 20.0% decline. Note once again the brutal economics of price cutting. Sales down 5.0%, gross margin down 20.0%.

Since the sales force is being paid as a percent of gross margin, the soldier's commission check falls by the same 20.0%. This commission plan is doing exactly what it was designed to do. It is penalizing the salesperson severely for not maintaining margin. With a 5.0% price cut there is a 20.0% commission cut.

The other variable expenses are 2.5% of sales, so they decline right along with sales. They are 2.5% of a smaller number so they fall by 5.0%. Fixed expenses, for about the 25th time (maybe 250th), do not fall.

The overall impact of the 5.0% price cut is to reduce profit from a $50,000 profit to a $37,500 loss. It is a staggering 175.0% decline. A margin-based commission plan helps a little bit, but not enough to even bother calculating. There is almost no commission shield that can be put between the price cutting by the sales force and company profit.

Draconian Commission Plan—*Almost no* commission shield doesn't mean *absolutely no* commission shield. The last column in Exhibit 28 demonstrates how such a shield might work. There will be blood on the saddle before the exhibit is done.

The only way to understand the last column is to jump around a little. The first three numbers at the top are the same as in the middle column. Namely, sales falls, cost of goods sold stays the same and gross margin declines sharply. At this point, time to head to the very bottom of the column.

The attack point is the pre-tax profit number. It has been kept exactly as it would have been in the absence of a price cut, namely $50,000. At this point the logic involves working back up the column. The first calculation is an accounting tautology. If gross margin is now $400,000 and profit is $50,000, then total expenses must be the difference between the two numbers or $350,000. That is the total expense number on the second line from the bottom.

The only task remaining is to divvy up the expenses into their three categories. Fixed expenses are a complete no brainer as they stay the same at $350,000. So, total expenses are $350,000 and fixed expenses are $350,000. A quick note for marketing folks reading this book—it's darned near all of it.

The other variable expenses are the same as they were in the middle column since sales are the same. That makes them $47,500. Commissions must be whatever is left over, or -$47,500. In sales manager terms, the performance review goes something like, "You write us a check for $47,500 and you get to keep your company car." The response of the salesperson is unprintable.

This is an incredibly brutal compensation system, but only for one type of salesperson. That is, the salesperson who cuts price as the only means by which sales can be made. The fact that such a system would cause them to leave is not that big a deal.

Finally it must be repeated that the salesperson that cuts price is much more likely to be a sales laggard than a soldier. The economics of such a double whammy will not be covered here to avoid cardiac arrest among the readers.

Okay, just enough of an analysis to require a quick shot of digitalis. A sales laggard who also cut price by 5.0% creates a one-person *loss* of $325,000.

There is a very short moral to conclude this section. In good times ineffective salespeople can be carried. In tough times they cannot. They cause profit problems that the hard-working, effective segment of the sales team can't overcome.

Improving Sales Force Performance

By design this book is 85% analytical and 15% prescriptive. Some of the 15% follows here. It will be limited to the areas where the profit analysis points specifically to related prescriptions. There are three such prescriptions.

Measuring Sales Territories—The exhibits in this chapter made the laughable assumption that all territories are created equal in terms of sales potential. In reality all territories are different; often by a lot. Therein lies a major problem in separating wheat from chaff in the sales force. You can't give the shaft to the chaff unless you know who they are.

Historically, it was extremely difficult to measure sales potential in a specific territory. It was possible to count the number of potential accounts and make some guesses about their needs. The analytical process was decidedly non-analytical, though.

The world is now in an era of "big data," for good or bad. All the author knows about big data is that it is big and involves data. That is enough.

With more granular information it is now possible to develop extremely sophisticated models identifying sales potential in individual territories. By knowing territory potential it is possible to determine if a specific salesperson is an 80% producer or a 120% producer. It makes a tremendous difference in the evaluation process.

Pruning the Tree—Once wheat has been distinguished from chaff by knowing the potential in every territory, some sort of follow-through is necessary. It is not the intent of this point to turn sales executives into newer models of "Chainsaw Al" Dunlap. One is probably more than enough. [23]

With better analytics it is possible to measure profit per salesperson with an amazing degree of precision. Distributors need to weigh the one-time costs of finding and training a new salesperson against the *perpetual* loss of profit from inadequate sales. Any such analysis will lead to occasional pruning.

---

[23] Both the successes and the gigantic failure of Al Dunlap are educational. See, for example, John A. Byrne, *Chainsaw: The Notorious Career of Al Dunlap,* Harper Paperbacks, 2003.

Pruning is not chopping, it is pruning. It still remains painful in small sub-divisions such as an individual branch. At some point it is unavoidable.

Continuous Follow-up—At the beginning of this chapter it was suggested that the sales job is one of the most difficult in the entire firm. It is also one of the most fragile. Because of the nature of the job it is very easy to become inefficient and not even be aware of it.

For example, if a salesperson makes five sales calls a day, that translates into 25 calls a week. During those calls there will be a lot of implied statements that the distributor's prices are a little bit too high. There may even be some direct statements to that effect.

During those 25 calls there will never be the suggestion that the distributor's prices are too low. It is one-way feedback on price. Eventually even the strongest-willed salesperson reaches a conclusion: Hey, our prices are too high. This is a classic example of the Stockholm Syndrome in action.[24] There are other manifestations as well. If a specific customer never buys a certain product category, then there becomes a self-reinforcing habit of never trying to penetrate that category with the account.

The solution is to train the sales force on an on-going basis. There is a tendency in some organizations to assume that trained once is trained forever. There is always a need to update skills and refine procedures. The sales force cannot be over-trained.

Running and Hiding for a Third Time—The author will now repeat a sentence already used twice before. In Chapter One it was suggested that firms not only had to deal with operational factors to be best of breed. They also had to have a market position that allowed them to run and hide from competition.

While it may not seem like it, developing a more effective sales force is actually a brilliant form of running and hiding. If the typical distributor has a mix of the good, the bad and the ugly in the sales force, there is competitive parity. If one distributor (let's call it you) can systematically develop a more powerful sales force, then more sales and profits will follow from that action. Competitors will know they are losing share, but not necessarily why.

---

[24] Psychological research suggests that only 20–25% of all individuals are susceptible to the syndrome. Kind of matches the percentage of salespeople who are Poor Performers.

Moving Forward to Chapter Six

The sales force is where everything comes together. With proper management, dedicated salespeople can help generate those needed sales, control expenses, and do both things with a reasonable gross margin.

This means that every one of the CPVs that have a major impact on ROA are in the fold. Seemingly, the profit yarn could end now and all would be right with the world. Unfortunately, there is still a "Say it ain't so Joe" moment in front of the firm.

Almost all of the profit actions to date ultimately lead the firm towards a larger level of investment to generate those higher sales and the like. Unfortunately, the funds available to support that investment don't seem to be adequate. Something will have to give before the entire profit project is completed.

Tweets® from Chapter Five

- Selling is an incredibly difficult activity.
- Many individuals do not possess the requisite skills necessary to function successfully in sales. Those individuals without the skill set may be delightful, hard-working people.
- The sales problems involve two aspects. The first is an inability to generate full potential from a territory. The second is a propensity to cut price more than is necessary.
- In both cases the firm suffers from not fully appreciating the *Cost of Goods Not Sold* issue.
- Firms must be a little more willing to spend the money to replace salespeople who are not performing. They should also be willing to train those who are left.
- With newer technology many of the typical problems of evaluating salesperson performance can be overcome.

A lot of what can be said about the sales force can be summed up in a quote by a different football coach (Bear Bryant): "If you want to make chicken salad, you better start with chicken."

6 Investment Strangulation

Of all the CPVs, the most completely misunderstood are the investment factors—inventory and accounts receivable. The misunderstanding arises because these are the only CPVs that must carry water on both shoulders. The firm needs more inventory and accounts receivable to avoid lost sales. At the same time, if it had less inventory and accounts receivable it would have more cash.

This double duty gets distributors knee deep into what Donald Rumsfeld cleverly described as "unknown unknowns." [25]

> ...there are known knowns; there are things we know we know. We also know there are known unknowns; that is to say we know there are some things we do not know. But there are also unknown unknowns—the ones we don't know we don't know.

The problem with managing investment levels in distribution is that the topic is replete with both clearly knowns and unknown unknowns. As it turns out, most of the things that lead to reducing investments are in the known category. The things that would lead to increasing investments are the unknown unknowns. The result is a serious case of investment strangulation.

In a feeble effort to convert unknowns into knowns and provide a balance between raising and lowering investment levels, this chapter is organized into three sections:

- **Cash is King**—An examination of the greatest example of conventional wisdom in the history of the free world.
- **The Unknown Unknowns of Investment Control**—A look at some of the hidden impacts of strangling investment levels.
- **Two Ways to Generate Cash**—A comparison of asset reduction programs and profit improvement programs.

---

[25] The quote is from a Department of Defense press briefing by Donald Rumsfeld in 2002.

Cash is King! (It is also another Profit Barrier)

Distributors suffer from a severe case of cash envy. Banks have cash. Microsoft has cash. Young punks running Internet companies that don't really do anything have lots of cash. Everybody seems to have cash. What do distributors have? They have their lousy accounts receivable and inventory.

Because of this seeming lack of cash, many firms made significant moves over the last decade to add cash. Those moves were only occasionally geared towards improving profitability to generate more cash. Instead, they were centered on reducing inventory and accounts receivable at the existing profit level.

Collectively, distributors adopted a common mantra—Cash is King. It is a wonderful slogan with four indelible characteristics. Namely, it is (1) short, (2) pithy, (3) easy to remember, and (4) stupid. Can this catchy phrase really be less valuable than typically thought?

This entire book has been counterintuitive. Why stop now just because the going is a little tough? Cash is King as it is typically applied has the potential to kill distributors.

As it turns out, kings come in all types and sizes. Louis XIV ruled France for 72 years, built Versailles, and was…well, never lonely in the evening. Louis XVI was beheaded. Both were kings. So is cash in the Louis XIV mold or in the Louis XVI mold? The prevailing wisdom is XIV. The author isn't so certain of that.

For distributors the discussion of cash poses three questions. First, why does the firm need cash to begin with? This is not as stupid a question as appears at first blush, incidentally. Second, how much cash will suffice? Third, how should that cash be generated in the firm? The first two topics will be discussed in the remainder of this section. The last topic is large enough to need its own section.

Reasons to Have Cash

Before attacking the reasons for cash it is first necessary to understand that there are two very different types of cash from a financial perspective. "Operational cash" is the money required to run the business successfully day to day. It allows the firm to pay its bills promptly, or at least eventually. Paying bills turns out to be an outstanding idea. "Investment cash" is the money that is available for non-operating needs, such as expansion of the business. Both are important, but operational cash is by far the more critical of the two.

Distributors routinely articulate four different reasons for wanting to have cash. One of them relates to the need for operating cash, the other three relate to investment cash. Note that attending a seminar where a financial guru shouts that Cash is King is not really a compelling reason.

Cushion Against a Financial Downturn—The most genuinely heartfelt reason to have more cash concerns operating cash. It is the need to be able to continue to operate in the face of a serious, but temporary profit decline. Such declines are most typically associated with a reduction in sales. The sales reductions are especially feared if they are triggered by sour economic conditions rather than by poor management.

In its most basic terms, cash is needed when bad things happen to good people. This is a commendable reason for cash. Even the cynical author likes this one. Despite its being genuinely loved by one and all, it has some limitations. In particular, it breaks down when pushed to its logical conclusion.

The reasoning behind this need for cash is that when the firm loses money (because of a lousy economy, never poor management), it can use up some of its cash to pay bills while it gets back on its financial feet. In doing so, of course, the firm will now have less cash.

If economic conditions are not a short-term problem, things have the potential to spiral out of control. The firm will keep losing money, keep using up its cash, and end up with no cash at all. In some cases this process can happen quickly.

If the process can be swift, then there surely must be a need for even more cash than originally thought. This need for cash is almost infinite. The truth is, though, that in terms of cash for economic challenges, distributors are looking at the wrong end of the horse.

Rather than worrying about the size of the rainy-day fund needed to survive an economic downturn, distributors should recession proof their businesses to generate profits in good times and bad. This is *not* a cheap shot, although it sure sounds that way initially.

If distributors could move to a higher profit position, they would have almost no requirement for cash to be used up during tough times. What distributors need is adequate profits to avoid the crisis to begin with.

The issue of recession proofing the business is a critical one. It will be discussed in the next section which covers how *much* cash is needed. For now, the logical flow is to first understand *why* cash is needed. Three investment-cash needs await the inquisitive reader.

Investment Income—With a lot of cash, the firm can invest those funds and generate a higher return on assets. In short, the firm can be both a distributor and a scaled-down version of Goldman Sachs. This concept is built around the idea that such funds will be invested in Google and Amazon at just the right time. They are never invested in Enron at just the wrong time.

Distributors run distribution businesses pretty well, despite the author's continued carping about the need to do better. Running a distribution business is a large enough job. It is probably a full-time job for most managers. Trying to run an investment concern on top of it defies logic.

Pay Down Debt—The author is a belt-and-suspenders type of guy when it comes to debt avoidance. Also, the empirical evidence clearly indicates that firms with less debt generate higher profits than firms with lots of debt. The idea of debt avoidance is an absolutely splendid one.

Paying off debt is a great reason to accumulate lots of investment cash. Of course, it is also a non sequitur. When the firm uses cash to pay off debt, it no longer has cash. It is a great reason to have cash for at least a little while, but not for the long run.

Buying Out Bozos—Finally, the pièce de résistance of this entire discussion: Successful businesses grow. Often the opportunities to grow come at the expense of competitors who did not buy this book.

This is the author's absolute favorite reason. However, it falls prey to the same poor logic as paying off debt. After buying the idiot competitor there is no cash left. Building a pool of funds for acquisitions over time is a great idea. However, it has nothing to do with cash for operations.

Reasons for Cash: An Assessment—None of the four reasons for wanting more cash is awe inspiring. Clearly, though, there is a need for an adequate amount of operating cash. That is, the firm needs cash to operate smoothly and successfully in a wide range of economic environments.

Anything beyond the amount needed for operations must be assigned to investment cash. How much cash, if any, should be committed to investment is yet another philosophical issue. The issue before the house now is exactly how much *operating* cash is required by the firm? Enough to be a king? Would you believe a prince? How about First Minister of Wales?

The Cash Needs

Distributors need enough cash to maintain their operations without interruption during seasonal peaks and valleys as well as during periods of economic strength and sluggishness. Too little cash is clearly a problem in this regard. In point of fact, too much is also a problem if the cash build up comes from hurting the business by being out of stock.

This is the crux of the author's monomaniacal hatred of the Cash is King phrase. It's not the cash that is the concern. It's how that cash is generated. With that incongruously-inserted rant out of the way, how much cash *is* needed?

There are two components to this question: (1) The amount of cash needed for seasonal patterns, and (2) the cash needed to ride out economic down-turns. The involve two, very-different analytical processes.

Seasonal Cash Requirements—Most businesses have at least a modest seasonal pattern to their sales. A few have significant ones. It is nice to stay afloat during the periods when the cash is trickling in rather than rolling in.

To look at the seasonality issue requires becoming conversant with an ob-scure financial ratio called the Defensive Interval. It is a "head for the bomb shelters" type of ratio. Despite that, it is extremely useful as a guideline.

The defensive interval, which is shown in **Exhibit 29**, calculates how long the company could survive if *no cash were coming in at all*. That definitely sounds like bomb-shelter thinking.

Exhibit 29
The Defensive Interval
Mountain View Distributing, Inc.

$$\frac{\text{Cash on Hand}}{(\text{Expenses other than Depreciation}) \div 365 \text{ Days}}$$

$$=$$

$$\frac{\$125,000}{(\$4,500,000 - \$137,500) \div 365 \text{ Days}}$$

$$=$$

$$\frac{\$125,000}{(\$4,362,500) \div 365 \text{ Days}}$$

$$=$$

$$\frac{\$125,000}{\$11,952}$$

$$=$$

$$10.5 \text{ Days}$$

The ratio is calculated by dividing the cash on hand by the amount of money the firm has to spend every day to operate the business. The figures in Exhibit 29 are once again for Mountain View.

Cash for the numerator was determined to be $125,000 way back in Exhibit 2. The denominator is daily expenses excluding depreciation.[26] The amount of depreciation has not been discussed previously in this book. Based upon the fixed assets for Mountain View ($1,375,000 according to Exhibit 2), depreciation of $137,500 is not unrealistic. There are very few 50-year investments in distribution.

The overall result is that Mountain View has a defensive interval of 10.5 days. This means it can rock along for 10.5 days with absolutely no cash coming in. This figure of 10.5 days could be sensational, neutral or terrible depending on seasonality.

For firms with no seasonal pattern of consequence, a defensive interval of 10.0 days provides more than enough cash. For firms with a moderate seasonal pattern, a figure on the order of 20.0 days is desirable. For highly seasonal firms, the figure should be more like 30.0 days. At the extreme of 30.0 days, Mountain View would need only about 6.0% of its total assets in cash.

With a well-established line of credit, of course, the firm could borrow when it runs out of cash. That would seem to make the defensive interval irrelevant. Even if the ratio for a seasonal firm fell from 30 days to 30 seconds, the firm could fall back on its borrowing capacity. However, if there is one thing to learn from recent economic challenges, it is that lines of credit come and lines of credit go. Better to have the cash and not need it than to ... well, you know the rest.

It is beginning to sound like the author has joined the Cash is King cabal. Actually, not. If Mountain View has no real seasonal pattern, its cash position—which is only 2.0% of total assets—is fine. That is not a lot of cash, but is still ample.

In point of fact, the $125,000 in cash is ample even though the firm owes its suppliers $1.0 million. Only as businesses become highly seasonal do they have a meaningful operational need for lots of cash. Few distributors fall into that category.

Mountain View may desire more cash than the 2.0% of total assets suggested above. That is well and good. It simply means the firm has exceeded its

---

[26] Depreciation is still an expense for the company. However it is also a non-cash item, so for short-run planning it can be set aside. In the long term it cannot be avoided, as trucks and other fixed assets have to be replaced when they wear out.

operating needs and is building an investment-cash fund for reasons known only to top management.

Economic Downturn Cash Requirements—The idea of how much cash is required to sustain the company in an economic downturn is an entirely different issue. It actually is not going to involve cash at all. Instead, it will rely upon that workhorse of financial ratios, the break-even point.

The break-even formula will not be discussed here. That compelling narrative has been exiled to Appendix C.[27] Instead, **Exhibit 30** will examine the results of a move to the break-even point by Mountain View.

As can be seen, if Mountain View experiences a 12.5% sales decline, its profit will fall to zero. This 12.5% figure is what is commonly referred to as Volume Sensitivity. A 12.5% sales decline produces a 100.0% profit decline.

Note that sales, cost of goods sold and gross margin all fall by the same 12.5%. The firm is buying everything at the same prices as before and selling everything at the same prices. It is simply doing it 12.5% less.

Exhibit 30
The Break-Even Point
Mountain View Distributing, Inc.

Income Statement	Current	Break Even	Percent Change
Net Sales	$20,000,000	$17,500,000	-12.5
Cost of Goods Sold	15,000,000	13,125,000	-12.5
Gross Margin	5,000,000	4,375,000	-12.5
Expenses			
Fixed	3,500,000	3,500,000	0.0
Variable (5.0% of Sales)	1,000,000	875,000	-12.5
Total Expenses	4,500,000	4,375,000	-2.8
Profit Before Taxes	$500,000	$0	-100.0

Fixed expenses are an albatross around the firm's neck in bad times as they do not fall, at least in the short run. Variable expenses, such as commissions, fall right along with sales. The net result is no profit.

---

[27] As a reminder, the break-even point calculation is not the only item covered in Appendix C. It also includes some useful examples of its usage in a variety of decision situations.

Listen carefully for the critically-important punch line. Conservatively-managed firms should be positioned so that they can withstand a *20.0% decline in sales* before they fall to their break-even point. A different, and probably better, way to say the same thing is that firms must be profitable enough to be able to look a 20.0% sales decline in the eye without blinking.

When sales are down by 20.0%, this profitable firm still may take all sorts of actions. Cutting payroll is one such reflexive action. However, the firm is not forced to take such actions. It can still operate, cover its expenses, not fire people who will later have to be hired back, and not forfeit a single dime of cash.

The need in a down economic period is not for more cash. It is for higher profit levels before the downturn hits. The 20.0% goal is not arbitrary. It reflects the fact that in the heart of the so-called Great Recession only very few firms (largely in construction-based industries) experienced sales declines in excess of 20.0%. With a 20.0% volume sensitivity factor, the company is prepared for almost any exigency.

The aforementioned Great Recession was the worst that the author has ever experienced. Even in the darkest of those days, though, some distributors generated stellar profits. Not adequate, not okay, not pretty good, but stellar.

Those firms also gained market share. The empirical evidence does not suggest that these firms started the Great Recession with more cash than the typical firm. They did, however, end it with more because they made piles of money during the recession while others made only a little or even lost some.

Ways to Generate Cash

At long last, the third and final point in the Old King Cash discussion can be addressed. That has to do with exactly how cash can be (and then, should be) generated.

Like a lot of other stuff in this book, the methods for generating cash can be dichotomized (sorry for yet another big word). Good or bad, right or wrong, yes or no. Understanding right or wrong and good or bad requires its own section and gets back to the theme of unknown unknowns.

The Unknown Unknowns of Investment Control

The colossal problem in investment control continues to be that many of the ways to generate cash also generate dramatic reductions in profits. Alas, nobody knows by how much. Let's call them unknown unknowns which this section will attempt to turn into known unknowns.

The issue is one that was addressed at the beginning of this chapter. The most common way to generate cash is to reduce the firm's investment in inventory and accounts receivable. However, since customers buy inventory and finance that inventory with accounts receivable, such reductions may lower sales. Given volume sensitivity (12.5% sales decline causes a 100.0% profit decline) lower sales will result in lower profits at a rapid clip.

To reiterate, inventory and accounts receivable are the only CPVs that are asked to do double duty: increase and decrease. Doing both at the same time seems a little hard to pull off. To understand the issue, consider **Exhibit 31**.

It looks at the two challenges associated with improving inventory performance. The same exact logic could be applied to accounts receivable. Mercifully, that will not be done here.

Exhibit 31 The Two Challenges with Inventory		
Issue	Provide Customer Service	Finance Growth
Measurement Tool	Fill Rate (Service Level)	Inventory Turnover
Ease of Measurement	Difficult	Very Easy
Calculation	Items Filled Items Ordered	Cost of Goods Sold Average Inventory
Mountain View's Performance	Not Known	6.0x
Implication	More Inventory	Less Inventory
Mantra	Can't sell apples from an empty cart.	Cash is King.

The "more inventory" argument in Exhibit 31 revolves around providing customer service. This idea was addressed earlier with the classic sales force lament of "You can't sell apples from an empty cart." Emotional, but still true.

The "less inventory" argument involves financing growth. If the firm has to keep adding inventory as it grows, this represents a real constraint on expanding the firm. Ideally, if the firm could use its inventory more productively, then it could expand without having to add gobs (or at least a lot) of additional inventory. Some will be needed, but not gobs.

This balancing act is agonizingly difficult to manage because of the nature of the two competing ratios that are used to analyze inventory performance. In Exhibit 31 those are the service level (fill rate) and inventory turnover.

The service level is the percentage of times the firm is in stock on things that customers want to buy. The inventory turnover ratio measures how effectively the firm is using its inventory. Since inventory turnover is easier to explain, it will be discussed first.

The time-honored formula for inventory turnover is cost of goods sold divided by inventory (ideally an average across the year). Since Mountain View had (Exhibit 2) $15,000,000 in cost of goods sold and $2,500,000 in inventory, its turnover is 6.0 times per year. That means it has about two months of inventory on hand (12 months ÷ 6 turns). That seems like a lot of inventory, so the argument for less inventory is fairly strong.

The reason that inventory turnover is the alpha dog in the pack of inventory management ratios is that it can be calculated with incredible precision. With Excel® (the author will get sued without the registered trademark symbol) inventory turnover can be calculated to 64 decimal places. It can be calculated yearly, monthly, weekly, daily, hourly or per nanosecond. It is there and everybody who gets an inventory report sees it.

In extremely sharp contrast, the service level is almost a mirage. It is virtually impossible to measure customer demand for products with great accuracy unless every customer request for merchandise is logged into the inventory control system. This renders the calculation almost meaningless from the start. A 95.2% fill rate was used in Chater Three. It was only a guess.

Further, sometimes different products can be substituted for items that are out of stock, making the calculation even more troublesome. Nevertheless, being out of stock frequently has the ultimate impact of causing customers to go away.

This difference in measurability (easy for turnover, really tough for service level) results in the combatants on one side of the inventory war completely routing the combatants on the other side. The folks who want to fill the cart with apples are being overrun by the Huns who want to empty the cart.

To gain some perspective it is useful to consider the profit and cash impacts associated with reducing the investment in inventory. The stopping-off point on that exciting journey is **Exhibit 32**. It looks at inventory from both an investment and sales perspective.

To avoid battle fatigue, this exhibit has been structured as a simple review of what was discussed previously. It is a combination of Exhibits 7 and 12. No need to look back, Exhibit 32 is self-contained.

Inventory Reduction—Mountain View's inventory is $2,500,000 so a 10.0% reduction is equal to $250,000 (Line 2). This immediately becomes

---

**Exhibit 32
The Impact of Inventory on Profit:
Two Different Perspectives
Mountain View Distributing, Inc.**

Inventory Reduction

1	Inventory		$2,500,000
2	10% Decrease in Inventory	[1 x 10%]	$250,000
3	Inventory Carrying Cost		20.0%
4	Increase in Profit	[2 x 3]	$50,000

Sales Loss

5	Lines Ordered		140,000
6	Fill Rate		95.2%
7	Lines Filled	[5 x 6]	133,333
8	Reduced Fill Rate		94.0%
9	New Lines Filled	[5 x 8]	131,600
10	Reduction in Lines Filled	[7 - 9]	1,733
11	Average Line Value		$150.00
12	Reduction in Sales	[10 x 11]	$259,950
13	Gross Margin %		25.0%
14	Variable Expense %		5.0%
15	Contribution Margin	[13 - 14]	20.0%
16	Decline in Profit	[12 x 15]	$51,990

cash. Since the firm only had $125,000 in cash to begin with, this is an absolutely wonderful occurrence. The CFO does a quick mental calculation on the size of the bonus check to be generated for achieving this feat.

From a profit perspective, the impact of an inventory reduction is associated with the Inventory Carrying Cost (ICC). The exhibit uses the still outrageously-high ICC of 20.0% (Line 3). Therefore, the profit impact is $50,000 (Line 4). Probably about the size of that CFO's bonus. Unfortunately, there are now fewer apples in the cart.

Sales Loss—The impact of fewer apples is virtually impossible to measure. Because the discussion is now into the realm of the unknowns, all that can be proffered in the exhibit is a classic "what if."

In this case, assume that the firm's customers try to buy 140,000 items during the year (Line 5) and the firm has a fill rate of 95.2%. These are the same figures that were used in Chapter Three and the result is 133,333 lines filled or groups of items sold (Line 7).

Assume now that because of a reduction in the number of apples in the cart, the fill rate falls to 94.0% from the 95.2%. A 1.2 percentage point decline is, admittedly, not a round number. Take a deep breath and ignore that momentarily.

With the same level of demand, namely 140,000 lines that customers really and truly want to buy, the firm either fills 95.2% of those or 94.0%. Ergo, there are either 133,333 (Line 7) or 131,600 lines filled (Line 9). The decline in lines filled is a miniscule 1.3%, or 1,733 lines (Line 10). With an average line value of $150, failing to fill 1,733 lines causes sales to fall by 1.3% or by $259,950 (Line 12).

With a gross margin of 25.0% and variable expenses of 5.0%, profit falls by $51,990 (the eagerly-awaited Line 16 which puts this exhibit out of its misery). It is a worrisome number in and of itself. At the same time, since the firm is telling customers to go somewhere else with greater frequency, it may be something beyond worrisome if continued long enough.

This discussion in no way suggests that the 10.0% decrease in inventory and the decline in the fill rate from 95.2% to 94.0% are related. One could very well happen without the other. They are independent "what ifs" at this point. All that should be noted here is that the 10.0% reduction in inventory and a 1.2 point drop in the service level have about the same impact on profit in the short run. The long run is still an unknown. It has been converted to a known unknown (lost customers), but still an unknown.

Having Your Cash Cake and Eating Your Profit Too

The above statement just broke the indoor track record for bad subhead titles. However, it does reflect an important point. Distributors don't need to find a middle ground between cash and profit. They need to generate both.

Before looking at that, let's retreat and review what customers expect from distributors. It will help position the narrative if we can understand what those suckers really want us to do.

The genesis for this discussion is yet another proprietary research project undertaken for a prominent trade association in distribution. That project was based upon the assumption that distributors needed to expand their service profile to lock in existing customers and find new ones.

In essence, it asked customers "What brand new, absolutely incredible services do you folks want?" The absolutely wonderful answer was "nothing!" That revelation did not keep the author from sending a bill.

Actually, not entirely nothing. Customers did say in no uncertain terms that no additional services were desired. However, customers did want distributors to perform better in two areas of *existing* services. First, a higher fill rate. Second, a greater assortment of products. It was an Edvard Munch-like scream[28] for more inventory.

The customers have spoken, darn them. They want distributors to carry more inventory. However, Mountain View has just the right amount of cash to cover seasonal fluctuations and can't afford to reduce its cash to invest in any more inventory. Time to generate both profit and cash.

The key to driving a higher fill rate and actually reducing inventory *simultaneously* gets back to a Ghost of Chapters Past: the Velocity Code concept. Now, instead of looking at velocity codes in relationship to pricing, the focus is on the velocity codes in relationship to inventory.

Exhibit 33 presents the item count, and the sales and inventory mix for four different velocity codes. The A+ group that was used in pricing has been combined with the A group. Taken collectively the A group constitutes only 10.0% of the item count, but represents 60.0% of the sales. They generate those sales while only eating up 40.0% of the firm's inventory investment.

Exhibit 33
Velocity Code Analysis for Inventory

Item Category	Percent of Items	Percent of Sales	Percent of Inventory
A: Commodities	10.0	60.0	40.0
B: Basics	20.0	20.0	20.0
C: Slow Sellers	20.0	15.0	20.0
D: Really Slow Sellers	50.0	5.0	20.0
Total	100.0	100.0	100.0

The B items were typical before, so why change a good thing now. They are 20.0% of items, sales and inventory. Boringly consistent then, boringly consistent now and forever.

The C items are a notch below the B items in terms of performance. They are about the same 20.0% of items and inventory, but only generate 15.0% of the firm's sales. Not a real problem yet.

The problem, and it is a big one, is with the D items. They are about half of the SKUs, so the firm's assortment is absolutely littered with them. Because they are slow selling they only generate 5.0% of the firm's sales. The rub is

---

[28] The iconic painting *The Scream* by Edvard Munch probably captures how many readers feel at this point in the book.

that they require 20.0% of the firm's inventory investment to do so. Clearly, they are candidates for elimination.

The opportunity for cutting inventory must lie with the D items. Oh, that it were an easy decision process. As a strategic matter, firms need to have some of the D items in order to build a reputation for always having everything that customers want. In that way, the firm still has the opportunity to sell the A items. Or as the old merchandising slogan goes, "Got to have some manure to make the roses grow."

The challenge with the D items has to do with the proper rose/manure ratio. The goal is to have a beautiful rose garden sprinkled gently with manure. It can't be a manure heap out of which is trying to grow a single, solitary rose.

Item Elimination—As a quick and dirty decision rule, any item that is *unique* in the product line and generates a reasonable level of sales volume should be maintained rather than eliminated. Unique means that the item is not functionally identical to another SKU that is an A, B or C item. Reasonable level of sales means whatever it means to the reader.

As a reminder from long, long ago (Chapter Four), D items that are maintaining that arbitrary reasonable sales level are candidates for price increases, not elimination. Such price increases will help offset their low sales level and also help the firm increase its overall gross margin percentage. It is a product category in which price increases are possible without causing customers to squawk. It is not one where lots of items should be eliminated.

The items that qualify for elimination are the duplicate ones. Any item resting comfortably in the D nest that is a duplicate of an A, B or C item might be dropped without negative consequences. In addition, any item that generated no sales volume in the last 12 months (yes, Virginia, there are such items) could probably be shown the door.

When (not if) these redundant items are eliminated—which is something really hard to do—then the money can be partially invested back into A items. It is the A items that inevitably need more inventory. Yes, inevitably.

Since people buy A items all the time, they are the only items that have the potential to experience out-of-stock situations frequently. What this means is that if inventory is too low or too imbalanced towards D items, the things that the firm is out of stock on are the things that customers want to buy all the time. It is a customer service nightmare. It is also why customers respond in research projects that they want a higher fill rate.

Migrating some inventory dollars from D items to A items will raise the service level and the sales volume for the firm. It will do so without taking any money out of cash and putting it into inventory. Two for the price of one.

There are some financial consultants who are much smarter than the author who argue that D items should be forcibly removed from the assortment in a mass vermin-extermination project. This is because those D items usually have very low price points and the cost of handling them is higher than the gross margin they generate.[29]

The author is not real keen on the "eliminate a lot of items" concept. That is even true for items where the firm doesn't cover its cost of handling the item. Customer service is the real king in distribution. At some point being the only distributor who can supply a left-handed veeblefetzer for a desperate customer will solidify the account.

Two Ways to Generate Cash

Since the phrase Cash is King has the staying power of Jason in the *Friday the 13th* movie series, it must be reckoned with. You want cash bubba, the author will give you cash. Just not in the way you would like.

Fundamentally, there are two distinct ways to generate cash. The first is the ritualistic "reduce inventory and reduce accounts receivable and hope that nothing bad happens" approach. This converts the unknown unknowns into known unknowns, but they are still unknowns.

Nobody can say with absolute precision what will happen to sales when inventory and accounts receivable fall. There is an inherent gamble. You pays your money and you takes your chances.

The other approach is what can be called the Microsoft approach to cash management. With this approach the firm makes so much profit that it faces the problem that Microsoft has. Where do we stack all this blasted cash? There is not only operating cash, but investment cash as well.

Sophisticated readers have already guessed that the author has a preference. That preference is revealed in **Exhibit 34** which serves as the denouement of the entire book. Okay, okay, the author went to school too long—the logical conclusion of the entire book.

Exhibit 34 presents a complete income statement and a partial balance sheet for Mountain View one last time. The first column is obligatory; where the firm stands at the present time. The last two columns make a number of assumptions that need to be followed step by step.

---

[29] See any of the recent writings or videos of Bruce Merrifield as an example. At last count, Bruce had 454 video clips posted on his Web site, which should sate the needs of the thirstiest item-elimination addict. They are available at merrifield.com.

Exhibit 34
The Financial Performance Impact of
Asset Reductions or Profit Enhancements
Mountain View Distributing, Inc.

| Income Statement | Current Results | ---Performance Next Year--- | |
		Asset Reduction	Profit Enhancement
Net Sales	$20,000,000	$20,000,000	$21,000,000
Cost of Goods Sold	15,000,000	15,000,000	15,645,000
Gross Margin	5,000,000	5,000,000	5,355,000
Expenses			
Payroll and Fringe Benefits	3,000,000	3,000,000	3,090,000
All Other Expenses	1,500,000	1,500,000	1,530,000
Total Expenses	4,500,000	4,500,000	4,620,000
Profit Before Taxes	500,000	500,000	735,000
Income Taxes (30% of PBT)	150,000	150,000	220,500
Profit After Taxes	$350,000	$350,000	$514,500
Balance Sheet			
Cash	$125,000	$943,750	$422,625
Accounts Receivable	2,187,500	1,968,750	2,296,875
Inventory	2,500,000	2,250,000	2,607,500
Other Current Assets	62,500	62,500	62,500
Total Current Assets	4,875,000	5,225,000	5,389,500
Fixed Assets	1,375,000	1,375,000	1,375,000
Total Assets	$6,250,000	$6,600,000	$6,764,500

Asset Reduction—In the middle column of numbers the first assumption is that the firm is generating the same exact income statement performance *next year* as in the Current Results column. This is how Mountain View will look after taking some actions. It is just that none of those actions are associated with the income statement.

The implication of this is that the firm will produce the same $350,000 of *after-tax* profits next year as it did this year. Further, the entire $350,000 will be reinvested back into the business.

Going down to the balance sheet, total assets (the bottom number) will increase by this $350,000, from the current $6,250,000 to $6,600,000. This is the same process as was demonstrated in Exhibit 15 long, long ago.

The final assumption for the middle column is that both inventory and accounts receivable are reduced by 10.0%. This is being done in a way that will not cause sales to fall, whatever that way is. All of the action with this scenario is confined to the balance sheet.

With more assets to begin with and less inventory and accounts receivable, cash has to increase a lot. It goes to a very comfortable $943,750. Cash is…you fill in the blank. The assumption is still that less inventory and less accounts receivable does not mean less sales. Call that assumption gargantuan.

Profit Enhancement—The last column demonstrates what happens if Mountain View's management gets "off the schneid" and actually changes the profit performance of the firm. This involves four actions, none of which are earth shattering:

- **Sales**—An increase of 5.0% which was the minimum improvement suggested in Chapter Three.
- **Gross Margin**—Increasing the gross margin percentage from 25.0% to 25.5% which should be attainable with pricing control. A stretch, but a small one.
- **Payroll**—An increase of 3.0% to generate the heralded 2.0% sales to payroll wedge.
- **All Other Expenses**—An increase of only 2.0% reflecting the fact that these expenses lend themselves to high levels of expense leveraging as sales increase. This is new information, but this is true.

As a result of all this, sales goes to $21.0 million (up 5.0%). The gross margin is $5,355,000 ($21.0 million times 25.5%). Payroll is up 3.0% to $3,090,000 and other expenses rise to $1,530,000, an increase of 2.0%.

The end product is an increase in pre-tax profit from $500,000 to $735,000. Profit after taxes becomes $514,500 (still a 30.0% tax rate). This entire sum also is reinvested back into the business.

With the reinvestment, total assets are now $6,764,500. There are some serious changes to inventory and accounts receivable to deal with before getting to cash. First, inventory increases at the same rate as cost of goods sold, not sales. It is not turning the inventory any faster than it did before, even though it should have eliminated some of those redundant D items. It is doing no better, no worse than before.

The investment in accounts receivable increases right along with sales. The firm collects at the same rate as before so the old Days Sales Outstanding (DSO) does not change. It is doing no better, no worse than before.

The net result is that cash is now $422,625. Only $422,625? What a piker the author is! In the Asset Reduction column, cash went all the way to $943,750. Yes, $422,625 is less cash than in the Asset Reduction column. However, it is a lot more cash than Mountain View started with. That was only $125,000. Seems like a very nice one-year improvement.

Plus, moving forward, cash will continue to rise every year if the firm does nothing more than simply replicate the new set of results. In short order (defined as three years), the profit enhancement approach will surpass the asset reduction approach in total cash generated. In addition, a continuing profit and cash stream has been developed. Welcome to nirvana.

Of course the firm could also keep reducing inventory and accounts receivable by 10.0% each year. At some point, though, sales begin to suffer. In particular, when both inventory and accounts receivable are reduced to zero, the ability to sell anything is diminished somewhat. At best, the asset reductions are a one-time or two-time activity.

Moving Forward to Chapter Seven

As part of a financial plan, the investment level in both inventory and accounts receivable would be best served if given benign neglect. Not outright neglect, but an effort to maintain the current level of performance and not try to dramatically lower either of the key investment factors.

The reality is that firms will have enough cash and can scream Cash is King all day long if they increase the profit that they generate. That higher level cannot be achieved if the firm is trying to cut back on its investments.

In the final analysis, having profit and cash requires a realistic financial plan. It doesn't require a detailed plan, it requires a realistic one. For too many firms the plan isn't realistic, but it sure is bloody detailed. Time to correct that little problem.

Crib Sheet from Chapter Six

- Distributors desperately want to have more cash.
- In the desire for more cash, it is useful to distinguish between operating cash and investment cash.
- If distributors have a defensive interval of at least 20.0 days (modestly-seasonal business), their short-term cash requirement is met.
- Distributors should improve their profitability to the point they are able to face a 20.0% decline in sales before reaching their break-even point.
- Reducing inventory and accounts receivable unilaterally is dangerous as most of the problems associated with such actions are unknown unknowns.
- With a proper plan, firms can generate both cash for the short run and profits for the long run, possibly in perpetuity.

7 Overbudgeting

The last chapter ended with the magnificent Exhibit 34 which demonstrated how, with some small changes, a distributor could generate a lot more profit than is currently being produced while simultaneously increasing cash. There would appear to be nothing left to say. That has never stopped Dr. Verbose before.

As brilliantly as Exhibit 34 tidied things up, it was simply a "what if" type of analysis. That is, some assumptions were made about sales growth, improving the gross margin percentage and the like. Those assumptions were fed into a basic financial model and a profit number cranked out the other end like a sausage. The number of "what if" sausages that can be produced is endless. There is a tendency to keep making them until one tastes good. This is not the way to plan the future.

In practice, the firm needs to have a budget that provides more than just an impetus to keep doing "what ifs" until something looks good. A realistic plan is required. This chapter will address that planning/budgeting process from two perspectives:

- **Managerial Profit Plan**—A suggested budgeting process with an emphasis on the role of the CEO.
- **Philosophical Concerns**—An examination of what is behind the budget and how the budget must be integrated into the culture of the firm. This sounds a little soft and squishy for the author's taste, but is actually pretty important.

The title of this chapter suggests that most efforts at budgeting are overly complicated. Truer words were never spoken. Trees are nice, but the forest is what really matters. From a top-management perspective the key to budgeting is a strong dose of "less is more."

Managerial Profit Plan

For top management the one key budgeting assignment is to take the heart of the budgeting process back from the CFO. The CEO of the company must prepare the framework for the budget and then turn the veritable plethora of incredibly boring details back over to the CFO. To brilliantly summarize this process: The CEO thinks while the CFO grunts.

If the CFO can help think, that is more than wonderful. It is serendipity personified. However, if the CEO doesn't do any thinking, that is completely unacceptable. Do Not Pass Go. The person responsible must be in charge. The ubiquitous phrase, "My accountant handles all that" must be exorcised.

The tone of the process is now set. The CEO is going to be in complete control and oversee the plan. With said tone set, time to pick out the tune. That is in **Exhibit 35**.

That exhibit outlines how the CEO must come up with four planned numbers. One of these, to resort to Star Trek terminology, will be the Primary Directive. The other three will support that directive. Four is the magic number. No more is required, but no fewer will get the job done. This is the skeleton of the budget that will drive the company. It is called a Managerial Profit Plan.

The function of a Managerial Profit Plan (MPP) is to determine where the company is going regarding profitability and how it is going to get there. Most of the how must be relegated to the next section of this chapter. For now the process is about financial numbers and nothing else.

Exhibit 35 reviews the planning process by providing a nostalgic farewell look at Mountain View. The exhibit presents the income statement for this firm along with total assets and return on assets. It conspicuously and intentionally ignores all of the details behind the total asset number.

Plan Profit First

The far left side of the exhibit presents the mandatory sequencing of actions in the plan. The very first step that needs to be taken is to set a profit goal. The rest of this paragraph is redundancy taken to its extreme, but it can't be helped: This is a decision for top management. It cannot be off-loaded to the accounting staff despite their self-professed brilliance.

Profit First Planning is a concept that says the very first item that should be planned each year is the amount of profit the firm is going to produce. This process overcomes the problem of profit simply being the result of a bunch

Exhibit 35
A Managerial Profit Plan
Mountain View Distributing, Inc.

Sequence	Income Statement	Current Results		Planned Results	
		Dollars	Percent	Dollars	Percent
2	Net Sales	$20,000,000	100.0	$21,400,000	100.0
	Cost of Goods Sold	15,000,000	75.0	16,028,600	74.9
3	Gross Margin	5,000,000	25.0	5,371,400	25.1
	Expenses				
4	Payroll Expenses	3,000,000	15.0	3,150,000	14.7
5b	Non-Payroll Expenses	1,500,000	7.5	1,565,150	7.3
5a	Total Expenses	4,500,000	22.5	4,715,150	22.0
1b	Profit Before Taxes	$500,000	2.5	$656,250	3.1
	Total Assets	$6,250,000		$6,250,000	
1a	Return on Assets	8.0%		10.5%	

Action Plan

1a	Increase the ROA to 10.5%.
1b	On the same investment, the ROA increase causes profits to rise to $656,250.
2	Increase sales by 7.0%.
3	Increase the gross margin percentage by .1%.
4	Increase payroll 2.0% slower than sales increases (5.0%).
5a	Calculate total expenses (gross margin minus profit).
5b	Calculate non-payroll expenses (total expenses minus payroll).

of "what if" exercises. It forces the entire organization to focus on how much profit must be generated. It is essential for success. For many firms it is also painful as it is so different from what they have done before.

Mountain View is planning to increase its ROA from the current 8.0% to 10.5% in Step 1a. This reflects a philosophy of slow, but steady improvements. In fact, for most distributors an improvement of anywhere from a 2.0 to 3.0 percentage point increase is a reasonable goal for a single year. Mountain View has demonstrated Solomon-like judgement and split the difference with a 2.5 percentage point improvement. [30]

Assuming that the asset base does not change (dumb assumption number five which is very close to the pain threshold of most readers) the planned profit for next year is $656,250. This is merely $6,250,000 in assets times 10.5% in Step 1b. The work was in setting the 10.5% number.

It should be noted that the idea of Profit First Planning (PFP) is controversial. Many argue that it is not possible to plan profit until sales, margin and expenses are planned first. Those arguments are prima facie wrong. The author just did it, so it can't be impossible.

The real argument is that planning profit first is illogical. This can be even more crudely expressed as "it's a dumb idea." The author's counter-argument is that the firms that do PFP seem to generate a lot more profit than those that don't. Go figure.

Planning the Critical Profit Variables

At this point a very logical and real question emerges, namely, "How are we going to do that?" The answer is not by developing a 50-line budget; that will come much later. The real answer is to focus intently on three critical items, what have been referred to as the Critical Profit Variables throughout this tome. Well, here they are.

Sales Growth—The first of the CPVs to be planned is sales growth. The one requirement to planning this item is to develop a conservative sales forecast. That means a sales increase that the firm is close to certain it can achieve.

---

[30] Only a simplified overview of the planning process can be presented here. Details on the process along with templates to actually develop a Managerial Profit Plan are provided in *Triple Your Profit!* by the indefatigable Albert Bates. It is an incredibly thin 77 pages and sells for a choke-inducing $39. Two points justify the price. First, it includes those incredible templates that can be used to actually understand the business and develop a financial plan. Second, the author has stated in this book that gross margin is the key to success. He is following his own sage advice.

In Exhibit 35 the firm is planning on 7.0% sales growth (Step 2). This figure includes inflation, growth in the overall market, any sales increases via order economics (see Chapter Three) and any gain in market share the firm may enjoy. It may be remembered (the author really hopes it is remembered) that the minimum sales goal should at least equal the inflation rate plus a safety factor.

Mountain View feels that it can move beyond the minimum because of market conditions and management actions. The fact that every reader of this book is bored senseless by 5.0% sales growth also was a stimulus to moving up.

The firm may well think a higher growth rate than 7.0% is possible given those favorable market conditions. That is fine, although the next section of this book will demand that the CEO tell the world exactly how this will take place. It is real embarrassing to admit it's all smoke and mirrors.

In the profit plan it is essential to temper growth expectations. The growth number is not a slam dunk. It should be an uncontested lay-up, though. Dream high, plan low.

It should be noted that the 7.0% is only for the financial plan. For the marketing plan the firm may well tell the sales force that the potential for 15.0% sales growth is very real. Such sales growth is a bluebird lying on the ground waiting to be picked up. It might even be low-hanging fruit depending upon the managerial analogy being employed.

However, the federal Truth in Profit Planning Act mandates that management admit that 7.0% growth is what is really needed. At the same time, since 15.0% really is out there, go get it! The marketing plan is a motivational tool. The Managerial Profit Plan is a real-world set of goals.

Gross Margin—The second of the CPVs is the change in the gross margin percentage. In planning gross margin, the same philosophy as was used for sales growth applies. The firm should plan on only a modest increase. Luckily, a small increase produces large results. The exhibit shows an increase from 25.0% of sales to 25.1% in Step 3. This is in the same neighborhood as a rounding error. Hard to get much smaller. Management would like to use a higher number but has been hit hard by price competition recently.

Gross margin continues to be what it has been throughout this book. It is the major driver of profitability. Even a small change is significant in its impact on the bottom line.

Payroll Expenses—The final CPV is the control of payroll. Here the sales to payroll wedge from Chapter Three rides in on a white horse once again.

Sales needs to increase about two percentage points faster than payroll expenses. This forces the firm to leverage payroll expenses effectively. Since sales increase by 7.0% in the example, payroll can only increase by 5.0% (Step 4).

Nothing Left Here but Us Calculations—The rest of the plan, pardon the phraseology, is simply plug and chug. In Step 5a total expenses must equal gross margin minus profit. There is nothing else it can be. Similarly, in Step 5b non-payroll expenses must equal total expenses minus payroll.

At this point the plan can be turned into a 30-line budget, a 50-line budget or even a 200-line one. What is essential is that before the final budget is set, management must put together a comprehensive plan that emphasizes profit improvement and control of the Critical Profit Variables.

Top management may be tempted to think that their work here is done. Let the underlings transfer the Managerial Profit Plan into a detailed budget. Like Alan Ladd in *Shane*, top management can ride off into the sunset. Or, in a more contemporary analogy, top management can head to the spa. Hold off one second.

There is still the little bitty (not sure why it is even being brought up) issue of how the firm is going to do this. There is no such thing in the MPP as "sales are going to increase by 7.0%." Instead, there is "sales are going to increase by 7.0% because we are going to do X, Y and the never-penultimate Z."

There are only three CPVs discussed here. Everybody in the firm needs to be tied into the plan based upon on how the CPVs are going to be improved. Developing this part of the plan and communicating it is harder than it looks.

Philosophical Concerns

Developing the plan was nice. It would be even nicer if the firm could actually reach the goals set in the plan. To help make the plan a reality, management must communicate in a way that too much of top management never does. Buy a Rudy Vallée souvenir megaphone on eBay and tell every employee who makes profit-impacting decisions what is going to be done.

This communication process has three components: (1) what we are going to do, (2) how we are going to do it, and (3) why we are going to do it. Miss any one of these and all of your reading so far will be wasted.

What—This should be extremely easy. All that is required is to review the key factors in Exhibit 35. Those are sales growth, gross margin percentage, payroll expense and non-payroll expenses. Everybody should know what the goals are in these simple areas.

If the reader will allow the author a personal vignette, it might prove helpful. The author once consulted (briefly) with a very large firm that did not tell anybody what its goals were. The company motto was more or less: Do better! It will probably not shock the reader to learn that the company never did do better. It was eventually liquidated at a major loss.

Some firms still hide many details from employees even today. This is no way to run a business. Time for more sage wisdom: If employees know where the firm is trying to go, they might actually help it get there.

The author is not arguing for open-book management. Some managers find it a great concept, others find it deficient. Using it depends upon the culture of the company. Instead, open-MPP management is being proposed. Every decision maker must know how much the company is going to sell, what gross margin will result and what the expenses will be. As a result they will know how profitably the company will operate.

How—This book has, by intention, focused a lot more on what to do than how to do it. However, it has at various points addressed the "how" issue. In discussions with employees the "how" is probably even more important than the "what."

As one example, in Chapter Four there was a discussion on producing a higher gross margin by re-pricing blind items. The inelegant term of "hose 'em" was employed there. It is areas like this where the "how" comes to the forefront.

The opportunity with blind items needs to be presented to employees. It must also be emphasized that the company really is not hosing anybody despite the author's crude comments. The company is carrying these blind items in inventory for a long time so they have them when customers need them. The firm must get rewarded for providing such an incredibly valuable service.

Some employees may not know gross margin from gross out. However, they can all relate to the idea of getting paid for what they do. Those financial numbers which the author relishes must be translated into actions that employees can understand.

If blind items are going to be the primary means of improving gross margin, then somebody has to identify those blind items. It is an integral part of the "how." Also, those key items need to be adjusted to the new price. This work is being done for a reason. It is how the firm achieves the "what" part of the gross margin improvement.

Why—This is where even some very sophisticated and well-managed firms fall short at the very last moment. There is a much greater degree of buy-in and a greater likelihood of goal achievement when folks know the underlying reasons behind the "what" and the "how." Without the "why" we are left with the immortal line from *Cool Hand Luke*, "what we got he'e is a failuh to communicate."

The process should go something like this: *Our company (not, my company) is trying to achieve certain goals involving the CPVs (the "what"). We are going to try to reach those goals through some specific actions which we all can help control (the "how"). If we reach those goals we will all benefit from the company having done so (the "why").*

That personal benefit can be defined in whatever mode management desires. It can be bonus payments, the likelihood of raises for next year or even the ever-popular "you get to keep your job." Whatever it is, the "why" component must be there.

Moving Forward to ~~Chapter~~...Life

Everything is so easy in a management book. The calculations work out precisely, the plan is set and reached and the dumb assumptions are forgotten or at least forgiven.

Life is so outrageously complicated in a real firm. The typical manager receives eleven emails and two voicemails while examining a single exhibit in this book. As a result, the details get in the way of the ideas.

At some point the ideas must come to the forefront. The concepts that were in the bullet points at the end of each chapter must be put into action. A good time to do that is right now.

Epitaph for Chapter Seven and the Entire Book

- Most distribution businesses can produce more profit than they currently do.
- The keys to reaching higher-profit results involve understanding and managing the CPVs correctly.
- "Correctly" means not following conventional wisdom unless that wisdom is based upon sound economic grounds.
- At some point the CPV analysis needs to be integrated into a simple, but well-developed management plan.
- That plan must be communicated to the people who are going to make the plan work. They need to know what, how and why.

Please note that the author never used the term "easy" anywhere in this book. Attainable, doable, realistic and achievable. Alas, not easy. As an offset to not easy: sure as blazes worth it.

Appendices

Appendix A: Documenting the Calculations

**The Impact on ROA of a 10.0% Improvement
In Each of the Critical Profit Variables
Covered in Exhibits 3 through 6**

Exhibit 3: Improving Gross Margin

1 Gross Margin			$5,000,000
2 10% Increase in Gross Margin	[1 x 10%]		$500,000
3 New Gross Margin	[1 + 2]		$5,500,000
4 Total Expenses			$4,500,000
5 New Profit	[3 - 4]		$1,000,000
6 Total Assets			$6,250,000
7 New ROA	[5 ÷ 6]		16.0%

Exhibit 4: Improving Sales

1 Sales			$20,000,000
2 10% Increase in Sales	[1 x 10%]		$2,000,000
3 New Sales	[1 + 2]		$22,000,000
4 Gross Margin Percentage			25.0%
5 New Gross Margin	[3 x 4]		$5,500,000
6 Variable Expense Percentage			5.0%
7 New Variable Expenses	[3 x 6]		$1,100,000
8 Fixed Expenses			$3,500,000
9 New Total Expenses	[7 + 8]		$4,600,000
10 New Profit	[5 - 9]		$900,000
11 Inventory and Accounts Receivable			$4,687,500
12 10% Increase in Inventory and Accounts Receivable	[11 x 10%]		$468,750
13 New Inventory and Accounts Receivable	[11 + 12]		$5,156,250
14 Total Assets Other Than Inventory and Accounts Receivable			$1,562,500
15 New Total Assets	[13 + 14]		$6,718,750
16 New ROA	[10 ÷ 15]		13.4%

Exhibit 5: Improving Expenses

1 Gross Margin			$5,000,000
2 Total Expenses			$4,500,000
3 10% Decrease in Expenses	[1 x 10%]		$450,000
4 New Total Expenses	[2 - 3]		$4,050,000
5 New Profit	[1 - 4]		$950,000
6 Total Assets			$6,250,000
7 New ROA	[5 ÷ 6]		15.2%

(Continued on next page)

Appendix A, cont'd.

Exhibit 6: Improving Inventory

1 Profit Before Taxes		$500,000
2 Inventory		$2,500,000
3 10% Decrease in Inventory	[1 x 10%]	$250,000
4 Inventory Carrying Cost*		20.0%
5 Increase in Profit	[3 x 4]	$50,000
6 New Profit	[1 + 5]	$550,000
7 Total Assets		$6,250,000
8 New Total Assets	[7 - 3]	$6,000,000
9 New ROA	[6 ÷ 8]	9.2%

Exhibit 6: Improving Accounts Receivable

1 Profit Before Taxes		$500,000
2 Accounts Receivable		$2,187,500
3 10% Decrease in Accounts Receivable	[1 x 10%]	$218,750
4 Accounts Receivable Carrying Cost*		10.0%
5 Increase in Profit	[3 x 4]	$21,875
6 New Profit	[1 + 5]	$521,875
7 Total Assets		$6,250,000
8 New Total Assets	[7 - 3]	$6,031,250
9 New ROA	[6 ÷ 8]	8.7%

* The Inventory Carrying Cost and Accounts Receivable Carrying Cost are discussed at length in Appendix B

Appendix B:
The Inventory Carrying Cost

The Inventory Carrying Cost (ICC) is an integral part of inventory analysis. It is used in a wide range of formulas, including those that determine order quantities. It measures what it costs the firm to have inventory on hand for a full year.

The ICC combines a lot of factors from various parts of the income statement into one metric. Since it is combining multiple items, a line for the ICC is not found anywhere on the income statement. It must be estimated from factors that are on the income statement or possibly imputed from items that are related to the income statement.

For example, the ICC includes the interest expense to finance inventory. If the firm actually does borrow money to finance inventory, then that portion of the interest expense line on the income statement that is associated with inventory is used. If the firm doesn't borrow money, then an opportunity cost is used to reflect the fact that if the investment were not in inventory it could be in interest-bearing securities.

The ICC is always expressed as a percentage of the firm's investment in inventory. An ICC of 20.0% would indicate that the total cost of maintaining inventory each year is equal to 20.0% of the value of the inventory on hand.

The major financial implication concerning the ICC is that the higher the number, the less inventory the distributor will want to carry. If the ICC were zero (it costs nothing to carry inventory), then the firm could carry an almost unlimited amount of inventory expense free. The only issue would be whether or not the warehouse is large enough to store it.

In contrast, with a high ICC, say 30.0%, every dollar of inventory reduction produces $.30 of additional profit. There is a strong incentive to reduce inventory. At various points in between 0.0% and 30.0% the firm may or may not want to reduce inventory.

The ICC is valuable in decision making. However, as valuable as it is, it is diminished by one serious issue. Namely, the ICC is habitually overstated.

This causes firms to be overly eager to shed inventory when they possibly should maintain or even add to inventory levels.

The overstatement is due to a witch's brew of uncertainty and self-serving intentions. That is, the ICC is partially overstated because of the difficulty in estimating the multitude of factors that go into it. Sadly, it is also overstated because a high ICC helps cost justify software systems that reduce inventory. Having made that very true statement the author will now be joining the federal witness protection program.

In order to make realistic decisions it would be nice to know just what should be in the fabled ICC. Five different items pop up regularly.

Interest—This is the single most direct factor that can be ascribed to the ICC. It is easiest to look at interest from an expense perspective rather than as an opportunity cost. Real costs for real people.

Since 1950 the prime rate has varied from 1.5% to 21.5% (who can forget those wonderful days). As of this writing, it stands at 3.3%. Many distributors borrow at the prime plus 1.0% or so. In addition, banks sometimes have "compensating balances" arrangements (park a portion of what is borrowed into a checking account). Given all of this an interest factor of 6.0% does not seem out of line.

Obsolescence—This would seem to be an easy factor to analyze. However, obsolescence varies widely by line of trade. For firms selling bananas, obsolescence occurs systematically and rapidly. For many electronic products the obsolescence rate may be astronomical.

At the other extreme, obsolescence for auto parts is extremely modest. It is still possible to buy a carburetor for a 1950 Ford (the author's first car; bought 20 years after it came off the assembly line). The price has not really gone down a lot as the carburetor has aged. There was a lot of interest paid, but no obsolescence.

Some items actually experience negative obsolescence as the value of the product rises over time. This situation is true for many commodities over the short run.

For most lines of trade (ignoring the extremes of obsolescence) this factor is probably in the 2.0% range. Individual firms should adjust to their own situation, either positive, neutral or negative.

Property Taxes—Some states tax inventory just like other real property. Some states, of course, tax everything, but that is another issue. The author will plug in 1.0% here. Readers must use their own rate, of course.

Shrinkage—At this point things begin to come unglued in calculating the ICC. The assumption that more inventory results in more shrinkage must be called into question. The logic here is that the more inventory there is on hand, the more that is either stolen or inaccurately accounted for. In reality, the size of the inventory has very little to do with shrinkage. It is the accuracy of the systems in place to monitor inventory that are the determinants of shrinkage. The author will grouse loudly, but will allow 1.0%.

Rent and Utilities—Starting here the logic is no longer possibly unglued, it is completely distorted. Supposedly, as the firm reduces its inventory the landlord will graciously lower the rent on the warehouse, and the power company (a benevolent organization if ever there were one) will also lower the utility bills. Unless the cuts in inventory are on the magnitude of 50.0% or so this is a bad joke poorly told. Put the author down for 0.0% if you don't mind.

Handling Expenses—One of the tricks of writing great Appendices: always save the best for last. The assumption is that as inventory is lowered (with sales remaining the same), the expense associated with handling inventory will also decline. That is, the cost of receiving inventory, inspecting it, putting it on the shelf, taking it back off the shelf and the like will fall.

In point of fact if the firm is reducing inventory without a reduction in sales, the firm is forced to place more orders with suppliers for a smaller amount of merchandise each time. The firm must receive more trucks at the back door, place more shipments on the shelf and process more purchase orders. If anything, this should be a negative ICC factor. A 0.0% factor will be used instead of a negative number only because the author is a great humanitarian. Even Albert Schweitzer would have used a negative number.

Implications of the ICC

The higher the ICC, the more the firm feels compelled to reduce its inventory. ICC factors of 30.0% have been suggested in some inventory control manuals. At present the ICC is probably closer to 10.0%, which just happens to be the total from the previous section. The author continues to be amazingly consistent. Not good, of course, but consistent.

A 10.0% factor is not inconsequential. It is just a lot smaller than most inventory texts would suggest. Throughout the discussion of inventory in this tome the author has used a 20.0% ICC. That was done (grudgingly) for two reasons.

First, a 20.0% ICC is not just Conventional Wisdom, it is absolute choir-singing Gospel. Going to 10.0% would cause too many readers to discount everything that was said about inventory in Chapters Two and Six.

Second, it was a conscious effort to give inventory reductions every possible benefit of the doubt. Even with a rate that is probably twice what it really should be, the economic benefits of reducing inventory are modest. At 10.0% they don't even approach rounding error in many instances.

The Accounts Receivable Carrying Cost

It is almost never discussed, but there is an Accounts Receivable Carrying Cost (ARCC) just as there is an Inventory Carrying Cost. Luckily, it is very straightforward and can be disposed of in one more paragraph.

The ARCC consists of interest (still 6.0%, see ICC discussion above), bad debt losses (anywhere from 1.0% to 2.0%) and the cost of hounding customers (another 2.0% or so). The author used 10.0% in the text which is probably dead nuts on (or dead naughts on for purists).

Appendix C:
The Break-Even Point

Break-even analysis is one of the most useful financial tools ever invented. However, it is plagued with the world's-worst name—break-even—so that nobody even wants to admit it exists. Who in their right mind simply wants to break even? The term has the same cachet as the Do-Nothing Party. It needs serious work.

In practice, the break-even point can be used in a wide variety of permutations to address such diverse issues as: (1) the amount of sales volume required to double profit, (2) whether bad debts are as bad as they are cracked up to be, and (3) how much sales has to rise when prices are cut. Essentially, it is an all-around useful ratio that should be in every manager's bag of tricks.

The Basic Formula

At its simplest, the break-even formula indicates at what sales level the company will generate no profit at all. This is negative from the start but proved useful during the Great Recession, so let's examine it briefly using numbers for the omnipresent Mountain View.

The formula requires knowing three bits of data which every firm should have at hand intimately. Those three items are fixed expenses, gross margin and variable expenses. It is nothing more than Accounting 101 at this point.

Fixed Expenses—In Exhibit 2 the fixed expenses for Mountain View were set at $3,500,000. It was noted that during the year these expenses would stay the same unless the firm took some action, such as hiring an additional employee. Hence the name, fixed expenses. Determining fixed expenses requires an estimate which causes some folks to give up on break-even analysis before they even start. Only a reasonable guess is needed, though, so don't let this issue be a barrier.

The figure for Mountain View is for a full year. However, the break-even point need not be for a year; any and all time frames will work. The fixed expenses must, of course, be for the same time frame as the calculation.

Gross Margin—Gross margin must be expressed as a percent of sales rather than in dollars. This should be absolutely no complication in using breakeven. Even with the worst accounting system in the history of the free world (iCigarBoxinthecloud.com) every company has to know its gross margin percentage. For Mountain View, the gross margin is 25.0%.

Variable Expenses—The variable expenses must also be expressed as a percent of sales. This is so simple it is painful, but, if the company knows its fixed expenses, then variable expenses are total expenses minus fixed expenses. Variable expenses divided by sales are variable expenses as a percent of sales. The variable expense percentage for Mountain View is 5.0% of sales.

The actual formula is shown down below. The formula uses a concept so rudimentary that even an HR Manager can remember it. Namely, dollars go in the numerator and percentages go in the denominator.

The idea is that the firm must cover its fixed expenses during the time period (we will use a year). That means that Mountain View must bring in enough revenue to just barely cover the $3,500,000 and not a cent more.

Alas and alack, the dollars that are generated in revenue aren't really worth a full dollar when trying to cover those fixed expenses. First pop out of the box, the much-maligned suppliers take a cut. For Mountain View the suppliers take 75 cents of every dollar, so the firm is left with a gross margin percentage of 25.0% of sales.

As is so often the case, it gets worse. The variable expenses take another 5.0% off of each dollar of revenue. This means that the fixed expenses must be covered with dollars of revenue that are only worth 20 cents (or 20.0%) each.

When the three factors are combined the break-even point for Mountain View is determined to be $17.5 million. The implication of this is discussed in Chapter Six, specifically Exhibit 30. (This appendix is devoted solely to formulas.)

$$
\begin{array}{c}
\textbf{Sales Required to Break Even} \\
= \\
\dfrac{\text{Fixed Expenses (\$)}}{\text{Gross Margin (\%)} - \text{Variable Exp. (\%)}} \\
= \\
\dfrac{\$3,500,000}{25.0\% - 5.0\%} \\
= \\
\dfrac{\$3,500,000}{20.0\%} \\
= \\
\$17,500,000
\end{array}
$$

Expanding the Concept

The basic idea of understanding the break-even point is valuable. However, the real power of the formula emerges when it is transmogrified into some other more interesting uses.

Profit Targeting—The quickest and easiest adaptation of the break-even point is to determine what sales level is required to reach a specific profit goal. This simply involves adding a profit goal to the numerator. Actually, the profit goal has been in the numerator all along. So far, however, the goal has been zero, which can't be described as stretch performance in most cases.

Let's assume Mountain View wanted to produce $1.0 million in profit, which is exactly double what it is now generating. Let's also assume that management at Mountain View feels they can do this with the existing fixed expenses. Ignoring the fact that management may be hallucinating, the calculation is really quite simple.

Sales Required to Reach a Target Profit

$$\frac{\text{Fixed Expenses (\$)}}{\text{Gross Margin (\%)}} \quad = \quad + \quad - \quad = \quad \frac{\text{Profit (\$)}}{\text{Variable Exp. (\%)}}$$

$$\frac{\$3,500,000}{25.0\%} \quad = \quad + \quad - \quad = \quad \frac{\$1,000,000}{5.0\%}$$

$$\frac{\$4,500,000}{20.0\%}$$

$$= \quad \$22,500,000$$

Making it Up with Volume—At present (according to Exhibit 2), Mountain View is generating $20.0 million in revenue and produces $500,000 in pre-tax profit. All of this is related to the underlying factors identified before: $3.5 million in fixed expenses, a gross margin of 25.0% and variable expenses of 5.0%.

If Mountain View were forced to lower its gross margin percentage to 23.0% in the face of blistering price competition, then the amount of sales it would have to generate to keep profit at the $500,000 level could be calculated easily.

Sales Required to Reach a Target Profit

$$= \frac{\text{Fixed Expenses (\$)}}{\text{Gross Margin (\%)}} + \frac{\text{Profit (\$)}}{\text{Variable Exp. (\%)}}$$

$$= \frac{\$3,500,000}{25.0\%} + \frac{\$1,000,000}{5.0\%}$$

$$= \frac{\$4,500,000}{20.0\%}$$

$$= \$22,500,000$$

Debunking Profitability Witchcraft—One of the most interesting uses of a modification of the break-even formula is to send bad financial analysis back into the gutter where it belongs. There is a lot of bad analysis, so the gutter will be very full if more managers understand break-even analysis.

One of the most outrageous examples of mindless financial legerdemain is in the question of "How much more will we have to sell to overcome this terrible atrocity?" This is most often seen when applied to areas like credit and collections where the terrible atrocity is a bad-debt loss. With the slightest encouragement bad debts—which nobody likes anyway—can be converted into an end-of-the-world apocalypse.

Suppose for a moment that Mountain View had a $20,000 bad debt loss from a specific customer who we can no longer locate. Candidly, we really should have been suspicious when he showed us his Kronos passport to establish a line of credit. Now we have to work our rear ends off to make up for that lapse in judgement.

The traditional approach (a euphemism for disgustingly wrong) starts with the fact that the firm's pre-tax profit margin is 2.5% (Exhibit 2). Then, the $20,000 bad debt loss is divided by the firm's 2.5% PBT to deduce that an additional $800,000 of sales is needed to offset the loss ($20,000 ÷ 2.5% = $800,000).

Two conclusions emerge. First, this is a misguided application of break-even analysis. Second, if it were true the firm should never offer credit to anybody.

Using the break-even formula indicates that the additional sales required is "only" $100,000.

Sales Required to Recover Profit After a Bad Debt Loss

$$\frac{\text{Bad Debt Loss (\$)}}{\text{Gross Margin (\%)} \quad - \quad \text{Variable Exp. (\%)}}$$

$$=$$

$$\frac{\$20,000}{25.0\% \quad - \quad 5.0\%}$$

$$=$$

$$\frac{\$20,000}{20.0\%}$$

$$=$$

$$\$100,000$$

Using the correct formula doesn't make the firm enjoy bad debt losses any more than using the incorrect formula. What it does do is put potential losses into proper context.

The break-even formula (in modified form) has a wide range of other uses. Managers really do need to become conversant with it in analyzing various decisions within the firm. Better decisions will follow.

Appendix D:
Making It Up with Volume

Exhibit 18 in the text generalized the increase in sales that would be required to exactly offset a price reduction to all of distribution, not just for Mountain View. That is, it measured how much sales would have to increase to keep the firm at the same exact profit level it had before the price cut.

To facilitate the current analysis, Exhibit 18 is reproduced here in its entirety.

Exhibit 18
The Percentage Increase in Sales
Required to Exactly Offset a Price Reduction
by Level of Original Gross Margin Percentage

Original Gross Margin (%)	Size of the Price Reduction (%)					
	1.0	2.0	5.0	10.0	20.0	25.0
5.0	31.6 %	94.1 %				
10.0	12.8	29.8	145.2 %			
15.0	7.7	16.9	59.4	369.6 %		
20.0	5.3	11.4	35.7	125.0		
25.0	3.9	8.3	24.6	71.4	1,500.0 %	
30.0	3.0	6.3	18.1	48.0	269.2	3,500.0 %

It was noted in the text that there were a number of assumptions underlying the exhibit. This appendix will address those assumptions so that the management of any firm can develop a specific "price cut/required volume increase" analysis.

At this point a warning sign should be erected: "Abandon hope all ye who enter here." Yes, this is another manifestation of the author's addiction to excessive hyperbole. However, the formulas get complicated in a hurry and the analysis of how changing assumptions impact the formula gets a little convoluted. Be forewarned.

As shown in the exhibit, the required increase in sales will vary with the firm's initial gross margin percentage and the size of the price cut. The lower the initial gross margin percentage, the greater the sales increase that will be required to offset it. Also, the greater the price cut, the greater the sales increase that will be required.

However, the size of the required sales increase will also vary with two factors that were ignored in Exhibit 18. They are: (1) the level of initial profit the firm generates, and (2) the ratio of variable expenses to fixed expenses.

Ultimately, all of these variables will be put into a break-even formula to determine the amount of sales that must be generated after a price cut. As a reminder, Appendix C suggested that the sales required to generate a specific level of profit is:

$$\text{Sales (\$)} = \frac{\text{Fixed Expenses (\$) + Profit (\$)}}{\text{Gross Margin (\%) - Variable Expense (\%)}}$$

So what can be so difficult about this warm, fuzzy little puppy of a formula? Lots, but before attacking the formula, it is useful to understand how the different variables in the formula lead to different resulting sales numbers. Specifically, there needs to be clarity on how expenses and the current profit level work through the formula.

Variable Expenses versus Fixed Expenses—Every firm has a different mix of fixed and variable expenses. As only one example, a firm that pays commissions rather than providing a salary to the sales team has made a decision about its expense structure. It will have more variable expenses (commissions) but fewer fixed expenses (salaries) than a firm that does not pay commissions.

This says nothing about the amount of total compensation to the sales force. With the same exact amount of compensation, one firm has lowered its fixed expenses by taking dollars out of salaries. This means it has increased its variable expenses by adding the same compensation expenses into commissions. Nothing can be said about whether this is a good or bad decision. It merely impacts the sensitivity of the firm to price cuts.

Firms with almost no variable expenses (but with offsetting fixed expenses) will not require as large an increase in sales to offset a price cut as would the same firm with lots of variable expenses. This is because each additional sales volume dollar will go entirely towards profit rather than towards a combination of additional variable expenses and profit. If sales dollars become profit dollars quicker, then fewer sales dollars are needed.

Profit Before Taxes—Firms with a high initial profit need less of a sales increase to overcome a price cut and maintain existing profit levels. That generalization, while true, requires some thinking about the break-even formula. The discussion will only be enjoyable for math majors.

In the break-even formula above, it should be obvious that when prices are cut the denominator will fall. Simply put, cutting prices will cause the gross margin percentage to fall. Consequently, the denominator must fall. With the falling denominator, the resulting level of sales required to offset the price cut will rise. That is true for every firm on the face of the earth. So far, so good.

If the firm generates a lot of profit initially, the numerator will be larger than for a company with, say, no profit at all. With a larger numerator, any given decline in the denominator (from a specific price cut) will not require as large an increase in sales on a percentage increase basis than for a firm with a smaller numerator. (Where is Mr. Spangler, the author's high-school algebra teacher, when he is needed?)

Let's quickly review and pretend we all understood what was just said. There are three truisms here. First, the more profit the firm makes initially, the less additional volume it will need to offset a price cut. Second, the more the firm's expense structure utilizes fixed expenses rather than variable expenses, the less additional volume it will need to offset a price cut. Finally, the higher the firm's initial gross margin percentage, the less additional volume it will need to offset a price cut, something pointed out in Exhibit 18 from the start.

At long last, we can return to the formula and calculate the sales required to offset a price cut for firms with any set of margin, profit and expense relationships. Alas, "it's always something" proves to be a true statement again.

Specifically, the word "New" has popped up in two places (Sales and Gross Margin):

$$\text{New Sales (\$)} = \frac{\text{Fixed Expenses (\$) + Profit (\$)}}{\text{New Gross Margin (\%) - Variable Expense (\%)}}$$

The problem is that the new gross margin percentage in the break-even formula requires its own detailed formula. This is because when prices are cut, the gross margin dollars on each sale and the size of the sale fall simultaneously. A rather torturous formula is required to determine exactly what happens to the gross margin percentage:

New Gross Margin (%) =
$$\frac{\{\text{Original Sales (\$)} \times [100\% - \text{Price Cut \%}]\} - \text{Original Cost of Goods (\$)}}{\text{Original Sales (\$)} \times [100\% - \text{Price Cut \%}]}$$

Voila! (Or as the author's family used to say down home, Wah lah). It's just that easy!

Okay, it looks like a complete mess. However, it can be plugged into a spreadsheet program with ease. Only six variables are needed: (1) the original dollar amount of cost of goods sold, (2) the original dollar profit, (3) the original fixed expenses, (4) the original variable expense percentage, (5) the original sales dollars, and (6) the percentage price cut.

A Few Thoughts Regarding Dr. Albert D. Bates

Al Bates has been consulting with distribution businesses since before most of the readers of this book were born. That means that he has acquired a great deal of insight and wisdom, but has lost the functionality of a lot of brain cells.

There is an old narrative about the stages in an entertainer's career. It applies to distribution consultants as well:

- Who is Al Bates?
- Get me Al Bates.
- Get me the next Al Bates.
- Who is Al Bates?

In short, Al has made a journey from the enfant terrible of distribution to the "Lion in Winter" of distribution. He likes to think he is still in Stage Two above, but is probably in Stage Three. Inevitably, he is heading towards Stage Four at warp speed.

In the journey through the four stages he has conducted more than 3,000 convention presentations, seminars and profit revival meetings. He has also written six books and more than 150 articles on profitability. Along the way he was one of the first recipients of a Ford Foundation Fellowship in Business Education.

Everything in the last paragraph is one big "So what?" The only thing that really matters in the bio sketch of life is the impact on other people. To Al's credit, a small number of companies have indicated that his work has changed their companies for the good. It would be nice if "a small number" could be changed to "a large number."

Plans are already under way to forcibly confine Al to the Home for Forgotten Consultants in Paris Island, South Carolina. If you will get off your duff and change your firm's profit structure, it would make his long days watching The Weather Channel in the Community Room much more enjoyable.